GETTING

PAID TO PLAY

An Inside Track to Professional Baseball

JAMES L. GAMBLE

GETTING PAID TO PLAY

An Inside Track to Professional Baseball

CONTENTS

Introduction 1

Section I: What is Professional Baseball? 5

Chapter 1: Understanding Professional Baseball 7

Chapter 2: Opportunities 15

Chapter 3: Professional or Semi-Pro 31

Section II: Let's Meet You Where You Are 39

Chapter 4: What to Measure 43

Chapter 5: Creating Your Plan 57

Section III: The Myths and Scams 67

Chapter 6: It Isn't "Drafted or Bust" 69

Chapter 7: Independent and International Leagues Are
Professional Baseball 73

Chapter 8: Just Because You're a Professional Baseball
Player Doesn't Mean You're Rich 77

Chapter 9: Pay-to-Play Leagues Aren't the Opportunity
They Appear to Be 83

Chapter 10: Professional Baseball Players Are Made,
Not Born 89

Chapter 11: You Can't Play Baseball Forever! 97

Chapter 12: Failure and Success Are the Same 103

Chapter 13: Divisions in Scouting Departments 107

Section IV: What You Need to Know (and Why) 111

Chapter 14: What Could Possibly Go Wrong? 113

Chapter 15: Leagues, Divisions, and Classifications . 117

Chapter 16: The Draft 121

Chapter 17: Free Agents 125

Chapter 18: The Independent Leagues 133

Chapter 19: The International Leagues.................... 137

Chapter 20: Salaries, Seasons, and Travel 143

Chapter 21: Taking Action 155

INTRODUCTION

$\sim\!\!\!\times\!\!\!\diamond\!\!\!\times\!\!\!\sim$

Y ou'll find that this book is broken into sections and the sections are broken into chapters. The design is to help you navigate the high-level considerations that come with playing professional baseball and then dig deep when you need to as you advance your career. I recommend you read this book cover-to-cover, but I also recommend that you re-read this book with a focus on the sections that will best help you advance your professional goals as a baseball player.

Here's what I'd like to share with you about getting paid to play baseball – and how I think you can benefit from reading this book.

1. **Section I** is all about the game because even if you think you know professional baseball, I've got things to share that I'd bet you never heard before. As I always do, I'll talk a lot about professionalism in baseball – what it means in general and what it means for the opportunities you may have in front of you.

2. **Section II** is designed to ask the tough questions that will set you up for success. I meet a lot of players who don't have an accurate picture of how they compare to other players, so I'll share the critical questions you need to answer honestly to determine an accurate picture of your skills.

3. In **Section III**, I'll tell you about myths and scams that exist in the world of baseball. Unfortunately, there are plenty to talk about, and I don't want any professional player to be misled, so I'll tell you what I've learned over the years.

4. **Section IV** focuses on the different ways you can play professional baseball. I share info about MLB Affiliates – everything from definitions and processes to the strategic approaches that can help players. These chapters will cover divisions, the draft, and even free agents. I also talk about International Baseball and Independent Leagues. It's my goal to help you understand what it means to play baseball internationally. In addition to leagues, getting signed, and understanding how baseball works in different countries, I'll also share what living and working as a professional baseball player for these leagues looks like.

As a professional baseball player, you'll have a lot of exciting choices to make, and I hope reading this book will allow you to expand the options you consider, your research techniques, and even the way you think in general as you approach your career in baseball.

Here's to your success!

—James L. Gamble

Author, Getting Paid to Play:
An Inside Track to Professional Baseball

SECTION 1

WHAT IS

PROFESSIONAL BASEBALL?

"Baseball was, is,
and always will be the best game in the world to me."

—Babe Ruth

I n this first section, I'm going to talk about what it means to play professional baseball. A lot of athletes in the United States think playing professional baseball means playing for one of the 30 existing MLB teams, but I'm going to use this section to show you just how many other ways there are to play.

Personally, I've worked in almost every capacity of the game all around the world. I've been on Minor League and international teams, served as a Minor League Pitching coach, been an assistant GM, and the Commissioner of the

Southeastern League. I've also scouted domestically and internationally. I've looked at the game from every angle so that I can share in this book what professional players need to know.

In addition to sharing a wide variety of opportunities that I'd like you to explore, I also hope this section helps you understand the different ways that athletes play baseball *professionally*. There are all kinds of ways that people can play baseball for exercise or just for fun – and there's nothing wrong with any of them! But when you're getting paid to play, you're a professional ballplayer. When playing baseball is how you pay your bills, that's your job.

Chapter 1

UNDERSTANDING
PROFESSIONAL BASEBALL

———— ⟨✕⟩ ————

"It's unbelievable how much you don't know about the game you've been playing your whole life."

—Mickey Mantle

P rofessional baseball players are the athletes who are paid to play – a simple definition I hope you'll remember as you approach your career decisions. While most people know that professional players are compensated, very few people realize how many ways you can earn a living in baseball. I'll start with the most common and well-known approaches and then work my way through some of the lesser known but still incredibly valuable clubs.

The MLB

Major League Baseball (MLB) is the most prestigious level of baseball played anywhere in the world. It is made up of the National and American Leagues and is played in the United States and Canada. Each season, there are multiple drafts, including the draft most people think about that occurs in the summer and the Rule 5 draft in December, where teams within both leagues build their teams and the World Series where the top team from both leagues compete in a seven-game series that results in a World Series championship team.

Minor League Baseball

Minor League Baseball has seven classes: AAA, AA, High A, Low A, Short-Season A, Advanced Rookie, and Rookie. Each Minor League team is affiliated with a major league team, and every major league team has at least one farm team. A Minor League or farm team is used to develop inexperienced players to potentially add to the affiliated major league team or to rehabilitate injured major league players as needed.

Independent Professional Baseball

In addition to the Minor Leagues associated with the MLB, there are also several Independent Leagues. The MLB may look for players in these Independent Leagues, although the teams aren't tied to any specific affiliate.

International Baseball

Describing opportunities to play baseball internationally can be a little challenging because there are emerging teams that some people may consider a viable option for a professional player while others don't. These emerging teams may also eventually be established enough to transition to a widely recognized option! I'll highlight the most common clubs in the fourth section of this book.

If a player grew up in the United States, dreaming about being a professional baseball player, then there's a good chance they saw themselves in their favorite MLB team's uniform, but as players mature, they look at professional baseball through a wider lens. There are so many ways to play, and – much like what athletes experience as younger players – each team has unique considerations that can potentially make it a perfect fit.

What does it take to play in these leagues?

I talk about each league in detail in the next chapter, but a common question I can answer in general terms is, "What does it take to play professional baseball?" There are common requirements that can be found in every league, even if scouting and team designs are different.

> » Your **athletic tools** (e.g., arm strength, foot speed, raw power and power production, fielding, and hitting) must be well above average when you play against non-professional players. If your performance is average – or especially below average – on a high school or college team, then it's unlikely you'll be signed to any professional league. The competition is fierce, and your game needs to be on point if you're going to go pro.
>
> » Your tools like **foot speed, arm strength, raw power and power production, fielding, and hitting** need to be at or above par for the league

you're looking to join. Those stats are available online, so check them out and see how you compare.

» You need what I like to call the **Compete Tool**. When you get knocked down, how quickly do you get back up? Do you show up early and stay late for practices and games? When you're not in uniform, do you still carry yourself as a professional baseball player and represent your team well? Professional baseball players have an internal drive that can be hard to describe, but I know it when I see it.

» You must view playing on a professional team as **your job**, and your sense of identity. No one playing professionally does so just for fun or in their free time. It's a commitment.

» The **financial incentives** associated with the league you're in have to meet what you need. I'm sure you'll be able to pay your bills if you're making a million-dollar salary in the MLB, but not every league pays that well. Make sure you have a way to make ends meet when you consider the average pay for the teams you're hoping to join.

For a lot of leagues, there are additional considerations that will require a high level of commitment and support from your family, too. For example, if you're interested in playing on an international league, is your spouse willing to move out of the country with you? If your team will be on the road more days than not, is your spouse okay taking care of your kids on their own? These are important questions to address early on as you consider a professional career in baseball.

If playing baseball is your job, what's it like to go to work?

Another common question that I get is what it means to be a professional baseball player daily. I'm sure you understand that it takes more than just showing up 10 minutes before game time to play, I also wanted to share some of the common requirements that may not be as obvious.

> » Depending on the game schedule, a professional baseball player will **attend team practices**. Of course, if there are several games scheduled in a week, downtime is used for physical rest and recovery instead of drills. But time between games is still used to discuss strategy, performance, and to increase mental toughness.
>
> » Players also often have **individual sessions with trainers and coaches** to work on specific areas they need to maintain or improve so that they continue to perform their best.
>
> » Some teams may have a **connection to the community** that requires their appearance for

promotional events. They may be asked to sign autographs or give interviews to boost engagement with fans and increase interest in the team.

When I share what it's like to be a professional baseball player, I try to emphasize how extensive the commitment is. You aren't a professional baseball player when you're in uniform, but someone else between games. You are *always* a baseball player. That may mean you can't take a trip with your buddies to Vegas because you have a practice that you can't miss. It might mean you don't take up a new sport in the off-season because the risk of injury is too great. It always means that you must think of yourself as a professional baseball player in every aspect of your life.

How do players know if they aren't cut out for professional baseball?

What if you read all this, consider the league requirements, and realize for one reason or another that this just isn't your path in life? There's nothing wrong with that decision! And you can still play baseball for fun if you don't play professionally. Loving the game doesn't mean you have to *live* the game. You have a lot of options, and if the full commitment required to play professionally isn't for you, then it's better to decide that early than to go through the arduous work and heartache for nothing!

You may also consider other ways you can be in the game without being a player. Some excellent baseball players become umpires, fitness trainers, or coaches. You may find that your specific skill set means your best bet is to work with players instead of being a player.

Wrap-up

If you desire a career as a professional baseball player, then I have a lot of valuable information to share with you. If you've already decided that you're meant to be a professional baseball player, then I've got advice that will help you identify the best opportunities. Wherever you are, I'm glad you're exploring the many ways that professional baseball players can succeed.

Chapter 2

OPPORTUNITIES

"Every day is a new opportunity. You can build on yesterday's success or put its failures behind and start over again. That's the way life is, with a new game every day, and that's the way baseball is."

—Bullet Bob Feller

In the last chapter, I talked about the different leagues that are potential good fits for players, but how are players supposed to decide what's right for them, and once they've decided on a few good options, what are players supposed to do to get noticed by the league that's right for them? Let's look at the best ways professional baseball players can make the right connections.

For each of the four ways you can play baseball professionally (major, minor, Independent, and international leagues), I've listed key considerations. I encourage you to also explore each league that appeals to you on your own, but carefully consider the source for any information you find online! If, for example, you're on a website promoting a specific league, it's safe to assume they'll be presenting information in the best possible light. It's always recommended to get multiple viewpoints, facts from unbiased resources, and the inside scoop from players who have played in each league!

To get you started, I've researched and shared the following for each league:

- » **General information (size, design, calendar, etc.)**
- » **Typical paths to getting scouted**
- » **Compensation and career length statistics**

Playing your best baseball career is all about finding the best fit, and there's a lot to balance. How much will you play? Where will you live? What's the compensation? Every player's experience will be different, but I can share some general details to help you identify the next steps.

What is Major League Baseball?

Major League Baseball is played in the United States and Canada. It is perceived as the most prestigious league (likely because of the high average compensation and media exposure), though there are certainly pros and cons, like any other league.

Playing in the MLB

There are currently 30 MLB teams, and no more than 26 players can be on each team's active roster. Each team has a 40-person roster of players under contract, but only 26 are eligible to play at any given time. Teams play 162 regular-season games: half in their home ballpark, and half on the road. The MLB season begins with Spring Training in February and can run through November if a team reaches the championship games (i.e., the World Series).

In addition to a long season and rigorous travel demands, MLB players also need to be comfortable playing in front of large crowds and potentially being the subject of discussions on television, social media, and other communication channels. Every baseball player needs a strong mental game, but MLB players especially need to be able to block distractions that could potentially negatively impact their game.

How do you get MLB scouts to notice you?

Typically, players who play Major League Baseball are selected through the amateur draft. Most often, they are already a high performer on a high school or college team and are then drafted to play in the Minor League. Many players have a successful Minor League career and never play in the MLB, but approximately 5% are called up to play Major League Baseball.

What kind of compensation and career trajectory can an MLB player anticipate?

MLB compensation is as good as it gets – the league *minimum* is around $500,000. While you often hear about top players receiving contracts worth tens of millions of dollars, the league average is about $4 million.

While receiving a few million dollars a year sounds like a deal anyone could make work, it's also important to consider how long the average player stays in the MLB. Like salaries, there are ranges, of course, but the average career is about six years. It's possible that a career in Major League Baseball could last a few games or 20 years – a smart player plans for both.

What is Minor League Baseball?

Minor League Baseball is a term used to describe teams that are in the Independent Leagues, International Leagues, and the teams affiliated with the MLB. Many people only think of the affiliate teams because Major League Baseball has a network of MLB affiliate teams that can be used for player development. Often, a player on an affiliate team will get called up to an MLB team, and then sent back down several times, based on their development and the needs of the MLB team, but that is only one kind of Minor League team in professional baseball.

Playing on an MLB Affiliate Team

There are levels in MLB affiliate teams, the highest being AAA. AAA (sometimes called triple A) is the highest, simply meaning that it's the league a player is most likely to get called up to the MLB from. Other levels include AA, A,

Class A advanced (High A), Class A (Low A), and Class A short season. Like so many other things I've been talking about, time spent on a team varies drastically for every player.

Different divisions have different schedules, but every level requires a full commitment from the player. Despite the lower salaries, the player expectations are high. Like the MLB, players attend practices and games, work with professionals to improve their game, and even sometimes have commitments off the field related to promoting the team.

How do you get Major League Baseball scouts to notice you?

Players are drafted by a Major League Baseball team and assigned to their Minor League affiliate. A common question is whether a person can try out for a Minor League Baseball team, and the short answer is that they can't. Being drafted out of high school or college is the most common way players join a Minor League affiliate team.

As strange as this may sound, while the affiliate teams don't hold tryouts, sometimes the Major League Baseball teams do. Technically, you could try out for an MLB team, who would assign you to their affiliate team if you made the cut.

There is also a different path for players who come from outside of the United States or Canada. It is possible for international players to be scouted and added to a Minor League Baseball team roster.

What kind of compensation can a Minor League Baseball player anticipate?

While there are a few Minor League players with million-dollar contracts, there aren't many. There are more that earn a modest $40K-$60K annual salary, and many make far less than that – as little as $5K a year. Minor League players on the low end of the pay scale must find creative ways to pay their bills while they work their way up to higher-paying positions.

In fact, the low salaries and lofty expectations associated with Minor League Baseball has a long history that continues to be battled in courts today. In 1922, the Supreme Court ruled that baseball was a "game", and not "interstate commerce" and therefore couldn't be regulated under federal law. In 2014, a group of players filed a class-action, wage-and-hour suit against Major League Baseball, requesting back pay for violations of federal labor law. In 2019, a ruling was made to allow that small group to expand and file a class-action lawsuit. This means a much larger number of current and former players can join the case, and Major League Baseball is more likely to make significant changes to their pay structure soon.

Court cases take a long time to bring about change, and there is a lot happening related to professional baseball right now. When considering pay, the best advice I can give you is to keep up with the news, so you're continually informed as changes come through. It's also a smart idea – no matter what laws change and when – to plan on working hard both on-and-off-season.

What kind of career trajectory can a Minor League Baseball player anticipate?

A professional baseball player could spend their entire career in Minor League Baseball, but how long will that career be? Again, there are so many factors to consider. If you do enter at the lower end of the pay scale, how long can you meet your financial needs? Are your skills developing in a way that allows you to believe you have a good chance of advancing? Have you suffered an injury? Like playing in any league, Minor League Baseball players should be continually planning for their future and making the best possible decisions based on the information they have available – always remaining open to new ways to develop.

A great resource for additional general information about Minor League baseball is MiLB.com. They provide an extensive list of frequently asked questions and answers that you may find helpful to read. For example, when asked about frequently occurring transactions in the Minor League, they provided a list of more than a dozen terms. The list includes various definitions like player recalled, contract selected, what it means when a player is assigned, optioned, or released, among other things! To read the full list and check out their other FAQs, head over to MiLB.com.

What is Independent League Baseball?

Independent League Baseball is played in the United States and Canada, like the MLB and the Minor Leagues, but a key point to remember is that Independent Baseball Leagues are not connected to either. Their independence from Major and Minor League Baseball allows them to play near MLB and Minor League teams without having to cut through any red tape.

Another fun piece of history associated with the Independent Baseball leagues and their lack of association with other leagues is that they were a huge part of growing the popularity of baseball! Because they didn't have to follow the same rules, they had more agility and could change locations as needed. Over time, they were major contributors to the development of the sport.

Independent Baseball leagues have come and gone over the years, but currently there are three that are active. Their league names and regions are listed below.

>> **American Association of Independent Professional Baseball** (Midwest, Texas, Manitoba)
>> **Atlantic League of Professional Baseball** (Northeast, Greater Houston)

» **Frontier League** (Midwest, Western Pennsylvania, Northeast, Quebec)

Playing Independent League Baseball

Independent League Baseball players spend a lot of time on the road, sleeping on buses and in hotels, but they also play the sport they love. Because scouts for Independent Leagues look for the specific talent they need on the team, a skilled player can find an active role in professional baseball and extend their experience.

How do you get an Independent Baseball team to notice you?

One of the biggest differences between Minor League Baseball and Independent Baseball is that the Independent Baseball League holds tryouts – and because they identify players through tryouts, this also gives the team a distinctive design. Since no one comes in with draft rankings, there is a stronger focus on what you can do to help the team win games, instead of how you can be developed to play Major League Baseball. That's not to say scouts don't find players for Independent Leagues – they do – but the focus on team goals makes the process noticeably different.

What kind of compensation and career trajectory can an ILB player anticipate?

Like Minor League compensation, Independent League players often make a few thousand dollars per year. The league is designed to support the players by matching them with host families or apartments to help offset the cost of living. Also, like Minor League play, career lengths and advancement in the league varies by player.

What International Leagues can you play for?

Professional baseball is played around the world, with established leagues in multiple countries. For example, in North America, leagues typically play in or near their home country, so players who join move with their families to a new country. At minimum, this means committing to learning a different culture, but it can also mean having to learn a new language or make other significant changes to their everyday lives.

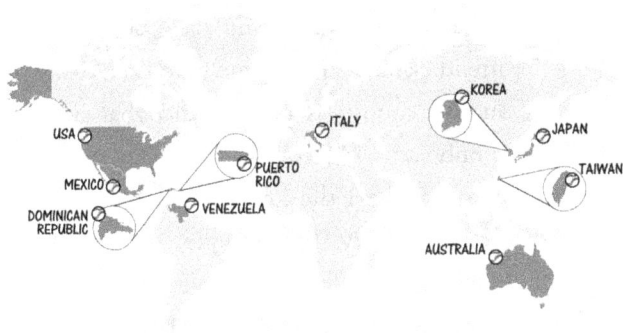

KOREA
ITALY
USA
PUERTO RICO
MEXICO
JAPAN
TAIWAN
DOMINICAN REPUBLIC
VENEZUELA
AUSTRALIA

Playing International Baseball

I've devoted an entire section to playing baseball outside of your home country because – not surprisingly – leagues within different countries will have a variety of different rules, regulations, and considerations. To start, I just want to share a few considerations.

» Are you interested in playing outside the United States? If you have an **interest in experiencing other cultures**, playing on a baseball team outside of the U.S. is an amazing opportunity. As a professional player, you'll be earning an income, but you'll also be with a team – people who can help you navigate a new culture.

» Joining a team outside the U.S. means **moving outside the U.S.** If you have a family, then this move must be a family decision. Consider whether your spouse has a job they would have to leave or whether you have children who attend school. For some families, living in another country is an experience that everyone is onboard with! For others, it may not work. Be sure to have the conversation.

» Every country has **unique strengths and challenges**. Before you agree to play in a completely new area, do some internet research about the culture! If possible, talk to people who have visited or lived there. Make sure there aren't any deal breakers associated with day-to-day living.

An opportunity to play on any professional baseball team is exciting – I just don't want anyone to take the leap without realizing how life outside the ballpark will be different than the U.S.

How do you get an International Baseball team to notice you?

Again, because there are so many leagues outside the United States, I'll cover the details in the section dedicated to international play, but typically, scouts find players to play internationally. This is another fitting example of why everyone interested in playing professional baseball should work with player advancement professionals – they can help make the right connections for players.

What kind of compensation and career trajectory can an International Baseball player anticipate?

Major League Baseball in the United States is the highest-paying league, but other leagues do pay well. An extra challenge when considering whether to play outside the United States is that you must do a little research about exchange rates, and the cost of living! Remember that while you're working outside the U.S., you'll be *living* outside the U.S., too. Your check may go farther or not, depending on the country you're in.

Some scouts find players for the MLB — or even the Minor Leagues — on international teams. Some players may choose to play internationally for a few years and come back to the U.S. on their own. Still others make their career in the new country they're playing in. Much like the other leagues, professional baseball players who explore teams outside their home country remain vigilant when considering the best opportunities available.

Another note about International Baseball is that no matter where you play, you'll likely have multiple countries represented on your team. People around the world grow up watching baseball in their own country and others. Their interest is gained at an early age; their talent is nurtured, and, when the time is right, they play – sometimes in the country that they live in, and sometimes in another part of the world. While many Americans grow up thinking that baseball is unique to the U.S, professional baseball players know that it is a sport played worldwide.

Wrap-up

There are a lot of options for professional baseball players. If you have a passion for the game, have developed the skills needed to play professionally, and have the family support to pursue any of these challenging paths, the reward is incredible. You can do what you love every day – how many people can say that about their careers?

As a player advancement professional, when I work professional baseball players, I encourage them to focus on three things: education, evaluation, and exposure. Chunking your continuous professional development into those three pieces can help you stay focused on the right things to advance your career.

> » **Education**: Keep learning about the game, the profession, and yourself.
> » **Evaluation**: Find honest ways to measure your progress in the areas that matter.
> » **Exposure**: Get in front of the right people repeatedly.

You may have heard the expression, "Success doesn't happen overnight." You can apply that same principle to education, evaluation, and exposure. A commitment to education isn't reading one book, it's continuously seeking out feedback and learning innovative approaches. Honestly evaluating your skills doesn't mean you assess your progress once a year, compared to the people around you; it means you're continuously measuring your progress and comparing it to the players in the leagues that you want to play in. Finally, no matter what we see in the movies, the right exposure isn't getting in front of one person one time; exposure that leads to a successful baseball career happens when you allow the right recruiters and coaches to see the skills you're bringing to the table, and this typically takes multiple tries.

In future chapters of this book, I'll share each of the leagues in detail, but I wanted to begin by giving you a brief introduction to each, and an opportunity to see the details side-by-side. Even if it feels like you're a perfect match for one specific league, I encourage you to read about all of them. You never know what opportunity may end up being your perfect fit, so having a little bit of knowledge about them can only be a good thing!

Chapter 3

PROFESSIONAL OR SEMI-PRO

"Catching a fly ball is a pleasure but knowing what to do with it after you catch it is a business."

—Tommy Henrich

I talk a lot about professionalism in the game of baseball. I'm constantly reminding young athletes that their actions off the field matter as much – and sometimes more – than what they do on the field. What you say, where you spend your time, what you eat, and who you spend your time with are all dramatically affected if you choose to pursue becoming a professional baseball player. Fans see you jog onto the field and think that's the start of your game, but they have no idea that your game started hours before that – and it will influence your choices long after the last out of the game.

Am I a professional baseball player?

You'll never hear a player who pays their bills by playing baseball in any league describe the work they do as "semi-professional." Someone who chooses their meals based on what will best support top performance, revs up their mental game through meditation and exercises to increase focus, heads to the ballpark hours early so that they can play a game of baseball that evening is the very definition of a committed professional. Playing professionally is a commitment to a lifestyle.

Playing professionally
is a commitment to a lifestyle.

Where did this idea of "semi-professional" players come from? The public – heavily influenced by television, movies, and social media – may think only of Major League Baseball when they think of professional players. I know, of course, that professional players can be found in countless other leagues, and those players show up every day and work just as hard. Here are a few points you can consider to better understand and explain to others what it means to be a professional baseball player:

> » ***Professional baseball players fail… a lot.*** Just think about what's considered a good batting average – 300. Batting 300 means you didn't get on base with a hit 70% of the time you were at bat…and yet you're considered a success.

That's because the design of the game dictates that professional baseball players try and fail often. Success is all about how you respond to your failures.

» *Professional baseball players know what to care about.* Have you ever had to "be the adult" in a situation and not respond emotionally when every fiber of your being wants to scream? If you've done that, you've had some experience in what it takes to be a successful ballplayer. Screaming fans, taunts from the opposing team, and the biggest challenge – your own mistakes or shortcomings – are hard to ignore. But professional players keep their cool and focus on what matters.

» *Professional baseball players are employees.* If you have a job, you show up on time and are expected to perform, right? Baseball players aren't any different. It can be deceptive – the work doesn't look like a traditional job! But they are paid by people who have expectations of them, and they are held accountable. This includes everything from following league requirements regarding appearance to performance during games.

What are the educational requirements of professional baseball?

While a lot of players do earn credit and even degrees while they play for a college baseball team, there aren't any post-secondary education requirements associated with playing professionally. You are likely to find, though, that successful players often find their own way of continuing their education. Sometimes it is in a traditional classroom studying fitness or sports psychology, but sometimes it's through reading the latest books related to their industry or attending seminars. Whatever the approach, education is often an important part of staying at the top of your game.

What should I do to get signed to the league that's right for me?

While I highlighted the path most associated with each league, there are some things every player aspiring to play professionally should know and remember. If you're looking for more guidance on how to secure a scholarship to play college ball, check out the first book I wrote with David Angeron, *It's My Time: Understanding College Recruiting and College Placement.* In general, here are a few things to shoot for.

» Preparation to play professional baseball **starts early**. Learning to independently develop the skills you need to be successful is a crucial step to complete.

» Securing a collegiate or professional baseball career doesn't happen just because you're a talented player or because you work hard. There is a lot to know, so I encourage serious players to **seek the support and advice of player advancement professionals** early in the process.

» Remember that securing a career as a professional baseball player involves **more than the work you do on the field**. The players I see who are successful are the ones who show up early and stay late, do more than what's asked, and understand that their talent, as well as their good choices, will help them secure their future.

If reading this chapter has opened your eyes to a few ways to play professional baseball that you weren't aware of before, I am glad! That was my goal. At this point, I recommend that you stay open to as many potential paths as possible. Keep playing your best game and seize opportunities as they emerge.

What do professional players do once they've retired from baseball?

Even though you're likely and understandably focused on how to start your career as a professional baseball player, it's normal to also wonder about what that entire career will look like. I encourage players to think about this as short-term and long-term goals.

Short-term goals can easily grab your full attention – both because they are so exciting and because they are the easiest to visualize. But long-term planning is important as well, so it's important to consider how long you can expect to play professionally and what you might do when you retire. Understanding your long-term goals can heavily influence the decisions you make every day, so it's critical to understand them, too.

Before I share some of the general statistics that are currently available for typical careers, I want to remind you that every player is different and that many things can throw a wrench into even the most well thought out plan. World wars or the 2020 pandemic are examples of environmental factors that historically impacted professional baseball careers. But injuries or a change in team ownership or coaching are more likely to change the length of your professional career. No matter what comes your way, it's important to make a plan based on thoughtful estimates while simultaneously being prepared for changes.

Wrap-up

As people transition to playing professional baseball, they may encounter people who don't understand that baseball is their career. And, if it helps, you're not alone! All kinds of professionals with non-traditional paths face the same kinds of comments – writers are questioned about their professionalism if they can do their work in sweatpants, teachers aren't taken seriously because they only work 9 months out of the year, fitness professionals are perceived to "hang out" at the gym all day. How do these professionals navigate the negative comments? They stand up for themselves and correct the misconceptions. But they also show up and act like professionals every day. Nothing stops criticism like *proving* someone wrong with your everyday actions.

SECTION 11

LET'S MEET

YOU WHERE YOU ARE

"The power of accurate observation is commonly called cynicism by those who have not got it."

—George Bernard Shaw

Every professional baseball player has a unique journey, so the first time I meet with players, my goal is to figure out where they're at in their career. There are all kinds of considerations that can help you accurately assess what your next steps should be, but there are also a lot of factors you need to honestly consider that may have given you a false sense of success.

Similarly, every team is in a different place on its unique journey. Every year and within every season, players come and go. Planned trades, unexpected losses due to injuries or slumps, and even how other teams have come together will influence each team's design. Because of that, teams are growing and evolving as much as players are. With so much movement and so many unknowns, how do players figure out how they can best position themselves?

When I talk to players, I like to give them a memorable way to think about who they should be in the eyes of their team. I tell them a little bit about myself, that I'm from the South, and that I love to cook a delicious meal and enjoy it with friends. You see, the story of how that delicious meal comes together perfectly demonstrates how recruiters and coaches look at their teams.

If I'm out and find a bottle of my favorite wine – the wine that will go perfectly with almost anything I make – then I'll buy a bottle. In fact, if I really like the wine, and I know my friends will enjoy it, I may buy a few bottles and put them away for the future. I value the wine, and I know it will eventually be a terrific addition to my meal.

But if I'm cooking for my guests, and I suddenly realize I don't have an onion that I *need* for the meal, then the experience is different. Unlike the wine – which I will casually buy because I know I'll need it eventually – I need that onion *right now*. I'm not going to shop around, drive to the store with the least-expensive produce, dig through an onion bin, or argue over price. I'm going to the closest market, grabbing what I need, paying whatever is asked, and hurrying home to use the onion that night. While the wine is great, and something I want, the onion is critical, and something I *need*.

In this section, I'm providing you with the questions that you need to ask yourself to get a clear picture of what you need to work on to become a professional baseball player. It's up to you to answer them honestly, and then create a plan to reach your goal. Along the way, I hope you remember that, although it may seem like a clever idea to be a fancy bottle of wine, those bottles sometimes get picked up too early and then left in a cabinet. The players who show up and work hard every day to develop their specific and valuable talents are the onions. Those are the players who meet a need that the team has.

Wouldn't you rather be an onion?

Chapter 4

WHAT TO MEASURE

—◇—

"In baseball, my theory is to strive for consistency, not to worry about the numbers. If you dwell on statistics you get shortsighted, if you aim for consistency, the numbers will be there at the end."

—Tom Seaver

The good news is that you can measure many of your skills and compare them to other professional baseball players. The following list will give you an idea of where you should start.

Measurements

Scouts use grades to describe where a player is at – and it's those common grades that help recruiters, players, and coaches share comparable information. Grades like the ones outlined below are used when assessing each of the five measurements critical to a professional baseball players success.

MLB GRADING SCALE

GRADE	DEFINITION
80	ELITE
70	WELL ABOVE AVERAGE; PLUS-PLUS
60	ABOVE AVERAGE; PLUS
50	AVERAGE
40	BELOW AVERAGE
30	WELL BELOW AVERAGE
20	POOR

MYTIME SPORTS

Each of these measurements can be improved and all the measurements are part of a bigger picture. Your goal should be to work toward being the best you can be – which may mean improvement in some areas and maintenance in others. View these guidelines as your opportunity to use industry insight to your advantage.

Targets

There are five measurements that every scout cares about. Luckily, each can be measured precisely, so you can determine exactly where you are, compared to your competition. Unfortunately, these skills can also be measured incorrectly, thereby leaving the athlete with incorrect information about their skill level. I want to make sure that you're setting yourself up with the most accurate information about your performance. I'm going to talk about each of measurement, and how you can be sure to secure the correct information for your plan.

» **Arm Strength**
» **Foot Speed**
» **Raw Power and Power Production**
» **Fielding**
» **Hitting**

Each of these measurements is important to different degrees, depending on the position that is being considered – that's why it's called a *target*. It isn't an exact science, but you need a starting point. These metrics will provide you with that. Your best bet is to know where you are in every category so that you can make any improvements you may need to be competitive.

Arm Strength

Arm strength is measured by a radar gun that calculates velocity. The need for each position is different, so there isn't one set number that scouts have in mind, but I've provided you with a few general guidelines. Scouts watch a player throw and decide whether they fit the position they're looking for.

Pitchers must consider arm strength differently. Scouts and coaches grade each pitch (e.g., fastball, curveball, etc.). Which pitches are graded – and whether deception, arm action, or other considerations are included – will vary, depending on who conducts the assessment. It's a little more to think about, but if you're a pitcher, then there's a good chance you're thinking that way, anyway. Just remember when you're tracking your progress to keep track of the variety of pitches, and how you're improving each one.

TARGET SCORES FOR
PROFESSIONAL BASEBALL

GRADE		FASTBALL VELOCITY
80	ELITE	97 MPH+
70	WELL ABOVE AVERAGE; PLUS-PLUS	94-96 MPH
60	ABOVE AVERAGE; PLUS	92-94 MPH
50	AVERAGE	89-91 MPH
40	BELOW AVERAGE	87-89 MPH
30	WELL BELOW AVERAGE	85-87 MPH
20	POOR	< 84 MPH

MYTIME
SPORTS

There are specific considerations for each measurement in professional play. For arm strength – and most of the other measurements – I strongly encourage you to evaluate how you measure your performance and if that measurement is biased in any way. Players can have a false sense of success if they use faulty equipment, inaccurately track their progress, or compare themselves to less-committed players. Be sure to check how you're gathering, tracking, and comparing information to make sure that you are being honest with yourself.

Arm strength is only one of the measurements scouts are looking at. But it is important, so if you want to improve your arm strength, here's what I recommend.

- » **Work with someone who understands the mechanics of the throwing motion**. Most communities have someone who specializes in improving the specific art of throwing and can provide detailed feedback for improvement.
- » Common and valuable advice is also to **improve your core**. With a stronger core, your throwing will improve.
- » **Practice throwing!** Did I even need to say that? Players tend to do what comes easily, but you need to force yourself to focus on the hard stuff sometimes.
- » Always **track your progress** so you can continue working with professionals.

Foot Speed

Foot speed is measured by clocking an athlete running a 60-yard dash. For accuracy, a stopwatch or a laser is used to record the time. A player who registers as a slower runner may not be of interest or they may simply shift their vision for you to another open position. Catchers, for example, don't need foot speeds that are at the top of the chart.

TARGET SCORES FOR
PROFESSIONAL BASEBALL

GRADE		FOOT SPEED: HOME TO 1B (LH HITTER / RH HITTER)
80	ELITE	3.9 SECS / 4.0 SECS
70	WELL ABOVE AVERAGE; PLUS-PLUS	4.0 SECS / 4.1 SECS
60	ABOVE AVERAGE; PLUS	4.1 SECS / 4.2 SECS
50	AVERAGE	4.2 SECS / 4.3 SECS
40	BELOW AVERAGE	4.3 SECS / 4.4 SECS
30	WELL BELOW AVERAGE	4.4 SECS / 4.5 SECS
20	POOR	4.5 SECS / 4.6 SECS

MYTIME SPORTS

Want to increase your foot speed? Here's what I recommend:

> » **Start sprinting** – that's what will increase your foot speed.

> » Like arm strength, **tracking your progress** is critical. The standard testing distance is 60 yards, so time yourself and keep track of your improvement!

» **Find an expert in your community who can assess your form**. They may identify a few simple adjustments that will increase your speed.

There are a lot of different athletes who track their foot speed and develop techniques for increasing their speed and agility. If foot speed is critical to your role on the team, whether you're looking to improve or maintain your numbers, add some variety to your training and learn techniques for improving your performance wherever you can.

Raw Power and Power Production

Raw power and power production is also measured by velocity, which is why you'll hear professionals use the term "exit velocity" when measuring an athlete's performance. Scouts watch for two things when they observe a player: how the ball went, and how much effort it took. They need to determine if the athlete exerted a lot of energy and if they can repeat their performance.

TARGET SCORES FOR
PROFESSIONAL BASEBALL

GRADE		HIT POWER (HOME RUN POWER)
80	ELITE	39+ HRS
70	WELL ABOVE AVERAGE; PLUS-PLUS	32 - 38 HRS
60	ABOVE AVERAGE; PLUS	35 - 32 HRS
50	AVERAGE	17 - 25 HRS
40	BELOW AVERAGE	11 - 17 HRS
30	WELL BELOW AVERAGE	5 - 11 HRS
20	POOR	< 5 HRS

MYTIME SPORTS

Raw power and power production are subjective. Every scout will see something different, and your grade could change from game to game, but don't feel frustrated by that. Remember two things. First, the professionals who are watching you are just that – professionals. They know what to look for, and how to assess a player's performance accurately. You don't need to worry about their skills; you need to worry about *your* skills. Second, different scouts may be watching a game, or the same scout may be watching you in multiple games. Therefore, you must show up every day and give 100%. I know you already knew that, but this is just one more reason that you need to commit to your performance every single day if you want to be a professional player.

If you'd like to improve your raw power and power production grade, here's what I recommend:

» **Work with a performance trainer** (speed, strength, agility) to improve your overall strength.

» **Track your movable size and strength improvements**. To be successful, you'll need to be quick and strong.

Fielding

Fielding percentage is measured by the number of times you correctly handle a batted or thrown ball. This includes successful work on the field (e.g., putouts and assists), as well as errors, which are bad for your average. The formula to calculate your fielding ability is:

$$\frac{\text{Putouts + Assists}}{\text{Opportunities (i.e., Putouts + Assists + Errors)}}$$

A scout will judge the infielder's hands, how soft they are, and their positioning, in addition to how well the athlete plays the outfield overall. Scouts will also ask themselves:

> » **Does this player cover ground well?**
> » **Do they take good angles to the ball?**
> » **Do they get good reads off the bat, and then get behind the ball and work through it?**

There are a lot of times when a scout will look at foot speed, arm strength, and fielding altogether. A scout may say, "We work with them as a center fielder because they're extremely fast, and they have a really good arm." They may move a player to the right side of the field if they have a below-average arm, or the left side of the field if they have a strong arm. Each measurement is important, but they should always be one piece of the bigger picture.

As you work toward the goal of becoming a professional player – and even after you have achieved your goal – you will continue to have opportunities to develop these specific skills. I encourage you to approach every practice and game as an opportunity to develop your fielding skills because these real-world experiences will help you improve your grade.

If you find that you need to improve your fielding skills, here's what I recommend:

> » Go online and **check out new techniques**.
> » Practice anything that requires **hand-eye coordination** (dance, juggling, etc.)
> » **Practice using both hands to complete various skills** (dribble a basketball with both

hands, throwing and catching a tennis ball with both hands)

» As always, **track your progress** to see what's working.

Hitting

Hitting ability is considered by many professionals in baseball to be the most important measurement, and it is the one that is the most subjective. Statistics are going to tell a scout what a player did and didn't do, but the statistics don't tell the whole story. There are always environmental factors – like who's pitching – that have the potential to work for and against a batter, so this measurement is challenging.

Because of this, a scout uses their professional judgment – their educated opinion – to make their decision. They look at several specific things to determine whether the player can compete at the next level.

» **Is the bat flat through the zone?**
» **Do they have a repeatable swing?**
» **Can they recognize and respond to a pitch?**
» **Can they manage their at-bat?**
» **Does the athlete have a balanced approach to hitting?**

Even though the measurement isn't as concrete as the others, there are still consistent things scouts look for. That list can be a great place to start.

TARGET SCORES FOR
PROFESSIONAL BASEBALL

GRADE		HIT TOOL
80	ELITE	.320 +
70	WELL ABOVE AVERAGE; PLUS-PLUS	.300 - .320
60	ABOVE AVERAGE; PLUS	.285 - .300
50	AVERAGE	.270 - .285
40	BELOW AVERAGE	.250 - .270
30	WELL BELOW AVERAGE	.225 - .250
20	POOR	< .225

MYTIME SPORTS

Sometimes, it takes a while for players to realize that hitting is a part of the game that improves with dedication over time. Often, when we think of great hitters, we falsely assume they were born talented. Some players may have a shorter learning curve (e.g., better natural coordination, more physical strength at a younger age, etc.), but they all work hard. No matter where you start, increasing your grade takes work.

Want to improve your hitting skills? Here's what I recommend:

>> **Repetition**. Spend some time at the batting cage!

>> **Find a coach that understands the mechanics of a swing**. Like foot speed, there could be something simple you can do to improve your game.

>> **Keep track of what works!**

The Compete Tool

The sixth consideration scouts will acknowledge is an intangible – and I call it the Compete Tool. Some people simply have something special about them that makes them a competitor no matter what the odds are. You can't identify that resiliency and commitment to improvement through a metric. You can tell some athletes based on concrete data what they can and can't do, and it won't matter. No matter how far behind they are or how many times they're knocked down, they'll always overachieve.

This intangible is the most sought-after tool, but it's impossible to define. To see it, you must get to know the player. What makes them great is their consistent success — even if they lack some of the other tools.

Wrap-up

When I look for talented players, I don't just want to know what they do during practice; I want to know what they do outside of practice and between games. How do they do at their jobs? Could they do better if they worked harder? Have they accepted being average in other aspects of their lives? That's what tells me if they have what it takes to be professional baseball players.

Chapter 5

CREATING YOUR PLAN

⬦

"People ask me what I do in winter when there's no baseball. I'll tell you what I do. I stare out the window and wait for spring."

—Rogers Hornsby

Once you've worked through and recorded the details from Chapter 5 that will help you determine exactly how you compare to today's professional baseball players, your next step is to figure out what you need to do to improve. You will never stop improving your skills as a professional baseball player, so you may as well accept these habits now.

As you create your plan and while you work on it, I also want to remind you to check in with the player advancement professional you're working with as well as any baseball professionals who have been supporting you in your journey so far. It's important to stay connected to player advancement professionals because it will help you stay top-of-mind with them, but also because they are most likely to identify resources that can help you. Others like your coaches or mentor can help, too, and provide you encouragement as you work your plan.

Personality Assessments

When player advancement professionals begin working with players, they need to learn about their personality. In the last chapter, I talked about the Compete Tool – the drive and resiliency every player needs to be successful at a professional level. But how players get there is different. There isn't one right set of personality traits that tells me a player has what it takes to succeed as a professional, but there are a series of things I like to know.

There are a lot of personality assessments on the market, but one that I use a lot is the mySkillsProfile specifically designed for athletes. The important things the assessment tells me about the aspiring professional baseball player's mental attitude includes:

- » **Confidence and Mental Resilience**
- » **Achievement Drive and Competitiveness**
- » **Sportsmanship**
- » **Interest in Power and Your Aggressiveness**

There isn't one category or score that's a deal-breaker, nor is there one that guarantees an athlete will be a success, but this kind of information can give me insight into the potential that each player has. From these types of reports, I can determine whether the desirable traits are what I am looking for and if the player is willing to develop the identified areas of improvement.

Adding to Your Plan

In the previous chapter, you took the time to assess your current skills – arm strength, foot speed, raw power and power production, fielding, and hitting. And it's true that you can't play at a professional level if you haven't accomplished those skills at the appropriate level. But plenty of athletes who had the right technical skills couldn't make it as professionals because they just didn't have the mental game they needed.

No matter which assessment tool you use, and which feedback you hear about your mental game, I'd like you to consider the areas where you need to improve. I'd also like you to think about why those areas might be challenging to change! Sometimes, understanding the reason(s) that you do or don't do something is the first major step you need to make toward making a lasting improvement. Consider the following examples.

Adaptability

I like to see if a player is adaptable, but not for the reasons you might think. A professional baseball career typically involves a lot of movement. You may be on an MLB team one week and playing on their affiliate the next. After that, you may be released and playing in an Independent League. Only an adaptable professional can manage that kind of career for the long-term.

But adaptability even more than how you navigate your career. Adaptability is how you navigate every practice, every game, and every day that you're a professional player. How do you take feedback? Will you try something new if your coach offers you advice? As the game changes, are you learning and changing with it? If your team needs to you step up, can you consistently evolve to be what's needed to win? Understanding how adaptable you are is what helps me see how you'll show up for work every day. Understanding how adaptable you are could also be what helps you understand how you can leverage or improve your skills to continue to impress team leadership.

Visualization

There are mental skills that feel like technical skills, so I want to share at least one for consideration. For example, what if you're asked about how often you use visualization to improve your game, and you realize that visualization techniques were never really part of your development strategy? Does the absence of that experience – or even a lack of interest in the technique – mean that you won't be successful? Of course not!

Visualization is an excellent example of a skill that you simply may not have much experience with yet. It could also be something that you only use minimally because that's just what works for you. It's a piece of the puzzle that gives me the full picture of who you are, and it can help you identify a new area that you may like to revisit as you develop professionally. Plus, by considering information like how adaptable you are, I can have a clear picture of what it might be like to help you develop the skills that you aren't currently using.

Managing Pressure

At every point in our lives, we've had to endure tremendous pressure. When we look back five, 10, and 15 years, we realize the pressure that we felt along the way wasn't the worst we'd experience; it just felt that way at the time because we didn't have enough to compare it to. How many games have you played in which the outcome rested on your shoulders? How often have you had a coach look to you – and *only* you – to find a solution? How often have you personally felt like you couldn't succeed at something, and that it would keep you from playing? Everyone has had different experiences, so everyone can describe their ability to manage themselves under pressure to different degrees.

Similarly, different people grow up with different life circumstances. One player may recall that the most pressure they ever experienced was a test they almost failed, which would have kept them from graduating. Another may remember when a parent became ill, and they needed to balance a job on top of baseball, just to make sure their family could pay rent. Both people have clear memories associated with their most stressful situations, but the outside world would easily identify one as more stressful than the other.

It isn't a contest – the person with the most stress in their life doesn't win a prize. But it is important for me and for each player to have an honest understanding of what kind of stress they have performed under, how they responded, and what kinds of pressure they can expect moving forward. Again, the idea isn't to say that a player who hasn't been in the position where the entire team was relying on them hasn't developed enough. It is to acknowledge your experiences and best understand yourself.

Awareness of Others

Working with a player advancement professional, you'll likely run into topics that may surprise you. Having and awareness of others, sometimes called empathy, is a skill people don't often associate with being a professional baseball player, but it is important. And specifically related to awareness, the ability to listen and respond to others is critical. When I work with players looking at a next-level career in baseball, they're often thinking about themselves – and I understand why. We think about our numbers, our goals, and our drive. But how we interact with others, how we show up for our team, and how well we can listen to a coach is critical to our own development.

Aggressiveness

There are also traits that may appear to have a negative undertone. Aggressiveness can be debilitating. It can keep you from connecting with others. It can lead you to make mistakes. But aggressiveness in an athlete isn't a terrible thing – when it's balanced. Do I want a player who intimidates their opponent? Yes! Do I want to work with driven, focused athletes? Of course, I do! Some aggressive feelings toward baseball, competition, and winning are exactly what teams need – if they are balanced by professionalism.

Putting It Together

Each of these traits is one of many that I talk to professional baseball players about as they plan their careers. Often, the mental considerations aren't one-size-fits-all. There are professionals who haven't yet had the specific experiences that will help them develop important traits. There are others who didn't have the best role models – and some who didn't have role models at all. Finding and cultivating these traits will prepare you for success as a professional baseball player.

In some cases, you may feel like you were lucky and picked up an important mental skill from a coach or parent, but don't discount the work you've done. If, for example, you find that you manage pressure well, that is something to be proud of. That is something you learned and earned, and it's unlikely that it's easy. It also won't last forever, so never make the mistake of believing that your mental game today doesn't need constant work. Recognize how far you've come and leverage your strengths to manage your career.

Wrap-up

To keep yourself organized and to keep from feeling overwhelmed, I recommend you complete the following steps.

1. **Record your honest results** from Chapter 5 on a spreadsheet or in a notebook, including your goal for each category.

2. **Assess your mental fitness** – with the help of a player advancement professional, coach, or someone who can help you access a reliable assessment for athletes and then interpret the results.

3. **Commit** to what you'll do to maintain or improve each category on a weekly basis. These commitments need to be measurable. For example, don't say, "I'll improve my foot speed." Commit to the actions you'll take (i.e., completing 5 specific workouts in a week) and any other applicable measurement.

SECTION III

THE MYTHS AND SCAMS

"Research is creating new knowledge."

—Neil Armstrong

As much as I hate writing it, there are a lot of myths and outright scams that professional baseball players get caught up in. When it's your dream to be a professional baseball player, it's easy to believe the things you want to be true. You're susceptible to hearing an easy solution and chasing it or being told you should give up your dream and believing it. I have two recommendations that will help you navigate your professional baseball career.

1. **Surround yourself with people you can trust.**

   Being a successful professional baseball player may feel like a solitary journey. After all, it's up to you to hit the goals you set. But just because you're the one doing the work doesn't mean you can't connect with industry professionals who will guide you through your journey and help you tackle the challenges you face along the way. Build your own team of trusted professionals that will allow you to focus your energy on your development by helping you answer the tough questions that you're sure to uncover on your journey.

2. **Educate yourself.** Throughout this book, I've shared ideas, goals, numbers, and all kinds of other things to consider. As you read each page, you've likely had thoughts about how realistic each idea felt, and the extent to which it really resonated with you. You may have even learned a few new things, or things that were contrary to what you've heard before. That's a good thing! Read and research what you hear. People may share bad advice and false information – even if they don't mean to. Even worse, some people will do it intentionally. Your best defense is to develop a fact-checking routine to make sure you're always working with the most accurate information.

In this section of the book, I've highlighted some of the most common and concerning myths and scams that I've heard about as a player advancement professional. This can be the start of your research. Remember, stay vigilant and verify what you hear about your career!

Chapter 6

IT ISN'T "DRAFTED OR BUST"

—∞◇∞—

*"Ever since I got drafted by the Yankees,
I've been working on my swing."*

—Aaron Judge

It may seem a little redundant to devote an entire chapter to debunking the myth that getting drafted is the only way to play professional baseball, considering this entire book is devoted to exploring all your paths and career choices, but it bears repeating. If you're getting paid to play, then you're a professional baseball player.

Let's take this chapter to recap your options and consider your approach.

> » **Make the right connections.** Wherever you are in your baseball career, you've likely met or will meet coaches, scouts, and player advancement professionals who will help you make decisions about your career. Finding the

right people to help you on your journey is critical to accomplish your goals.

» **Consider all the levels.** This book has given you a lot of information about all the levels of professional baseball, including what schedules and pay you can expect. You're now armed with all the information you need to prepare yourself for the different choices that will come your way, but don't make the mistake of committing to one path – even if you do choose the path you prefer. Educate yourself and stay open to MLB affiliates, Independent Leagues, and International Baseball!

» **Honestly evaluate where you are.** Using feedback from the trusted professionals you're working with, evaluate your skills, including your mental game. What do you need to work on to compete at your goal level? What are the steps you need to take to reach that level?

» **Create your plan.** Ideally, if you're working with a player advancement professional, then you've got someone in your corner to help you measure and keep track of your progress. If not, a good place to start is the skills list in this book. When you're creating your plan, just remember to include your physical and mental game and to measure or get a second opinion on everything. The best thing you can do for yourself is to start with an honest assessment of where you are – even if it uncovers challenges that may initially feel frustrating.

Wrap-up

Is it drafted or bust? Not even close. In fact, if you think it is, there's a good chance you don't have the mental game yet to play professional baseball. It's a competitive business, but there are also a lot of ways to follow your passion!

Chapter 7

INDEPENDENT AND INTERNATIONAL LEAGUES ARE PROFESSIONAL BASEBALL

*"If you're going to play at all, you're out to win.
Baseball, board games, Jeopardy, I hate to lose."*

—Derek Jeter

A lot of aspiring professional baseball players grow up watching Major League Baseball, so the MLB becomes the only version of professional baseball that they know and understand. They learn about MLB teams, and their Minor League affiliates. They follow MLB players and learn about how they made it to the big leagues. However, despite all these wonderful experiences, our understanding of professional baseball is missing a lot of information.

Professional baseball takes many different forms around the world. Any instance in which a coaching staff has selected a player for their talents and pays them to play baseball is professional play! Just because the team isn't an MLB or MLB-affiliate team doesn't mean the teams aren't made up of professional players.

Where did this misconception come from?

As I already said, this idea that every professional player needs to be in the MLB, or an affiliate, comes at least in part from our own experiences as young baseball fans. What we see when we're growing up tends to be what sticks in our minds. If your family sat around the TV and watched MLB games, but they didn't take trips out to see Independent League games, then you would have been left with the idea that there is only one kind of professional baseball.

There's also a good chance that hanging out with other baseball players, that idea was reinforced because you all probably talked about playing in the big leagues! It's fun and exciting–I get the appeal. I had those dreams, too. But sometimes the dream of knocking a homerun out of the park while thousands of fans in a major league ballpark cheer can make us forget the real reason professional baseball players are successful. Their drive and commitment to their own development and success comes from their passion for the game, not from their desire for fame.

Take a fresh look at what you know about baseball, and all the professional baseball players that you've heard talk about the game. If you've met some in person, then that's awesome! Consider those conversations. But even if you haven't, watch interviews and read articles in which players talk about their games and their careers. Listen to what they emphasize, and you will hear professional baseball players in any league talking about the same things: their commitment to mastering the game, how their team works together, and what they are personally working to improve.

Why is it important that you understand what professional baseball really is?

The sooner you understand all the ways you can become a professional baseball player, the sooner you can create a detailed plan to play ball as your career. Think about any other career that your friends or family members have. If someone were passionate about being a teacher, but they only wanted to teach the third grade, and only in a small town, then how long would it take them to find a job? If someone else had a knack for numbers and decided to pursue accounting, but they only wanted to work for a Fortune 500 company, and they were only willing to be a staff accountant, then could they land their dream job? Of course, it's possible – the world needs third-grade teachers and staff accountants – but their narrow view of their dream job would make it extremely difficult to start their career, and they'd likely miss out on amazing opportunities along the way.

If you get up every day with the mindset that you're working toward getting drafted, then you will miss amazing opportunities to play professional baseball. If you only think about your next step landing you a spot on a 40-man roster, then you won't capitalize on the other incredible opportunities to play on independent teams. Playing professional baseball can happen so many ways, and one of the best things a player can do for their own career is change their mindset. Realizing that professional baseball has many paths is a critical first step on your journey.

Wrap-up

It's good to be flexible and open to ideas in any way that you can be. Talking to professionals who play in and manage different leagues, working with recruiting professionals to make sure you see and understand your options, and thinking about your choices as career decisions will help you maximize the opportunities to play professional baseball that come your way.

Chapter 8

JUST BECAUSE YOU'RE A PROFESSIONAL BASEBALL PLAYER DOESN'T MEAN YOU'RE RICH

"I could have played another year, but I would have been playing for the money, and baseball deserves better than that."

—George Brett

It's true that our main goal for this book was to share with you all the different ways professional baseball players get paid to play the sport they love. But playing professionally doesn't guarantee that you'll be taking home a million-dollar paycheck. In fact, as you saw in the other chapters, there are a lot of ways that you're paid to play that won't pay enough for you to pay your bills all year long.

In this chapter, I'm going to cover how professional baseball players make their salaries work for them, both by making smart choices in the off-season and by working with baseball professionals to draft a plan for the season that will meet their financial goals.

Find Seasonal Employment in the Off-Season

There are a lot of companies happy to hire reliable, hard-working employees for short periods of time. During the off-season, consider working as many hours you can with through opportunities like:

- » **Rideshare Services** (e.g., Uber or Lyft)
- » **Food Delivery Services** (e.g., DoorDash or local restaurants)
- » **Gyms or Fitness Studios** (e.g., working at the front desk or cleaning)
- » **Coaching or Private Lessons** (e.g., to young athletes)

While I encourage you to make the most of the off-season so that you can build your savings, it's also important to leave time to keep your skills sharp. Make sure that you keep time on your calendar for exercise and continue your healthy eating habits when you aren't checking in with your coach every day!

Get Creative with Rent

A significant expense for anyone is their rent or mortgage, so cutting your rent expenses is a good way to start saving money. Here are some of the best options I've seen.

> » **Stay with teammates.** Whether you're playing or not, there's a good chance your teammates are in the same financial boat you are. See if there is an opportunity to share housing.
>
> » **Stay with family when you're not on the road.** Do your parents still have an extra room where you can crash? Will your brother let you couch-surf in his basement during the off-season?
>
> » **Look for a way to swap work for rent.** Assuming this won't interfere with any part of your team commitment, you may be able to help someone out and secure a place to stay at the same time. For example, someone may be looking for a long-term house-sitter while they travel.

Sharing a space with other people – or even moving every year as new opportunities become available – isn't ideal, but when you think about how much you can save on rent, you may decide it's worth it.

Maximize Your Per Diem (and any other money you make)

Sometimes making your finances work is as simple as educating yourself about the everyday choices that can save you money. Take the per diem and salary you get for playing during the baseball season and stretch it out following these few tips.

» **Write out your budget – and stick to it.** Just thinking about making better financial decisions is unlikely to change your behavior. However, if you write your budget down and display it somewhere so it stays top-of-mind, you're more likely to avoid making unnecessary purchases.

» **Cook at home.** You don't have to completely deprive yourself of fun but limiting how often you go out to eat can add up to huge savings. If your friends want to go out to dinner, then try suggesting a potluck dinner on someone's patio instead. You'll realize quickly that your time with friends is what matters, not the food you're eating!

» Always **look for free and low-cost alternatives**. You have access to more discounted pricing than you realize – and all you have to do is ask! Check with your insurance provider, or any group you are affiliated with (e.g., religious groups, state/district programs, etc.) to see what discounts you're eligible for, and what free resources you can access. Rent your movies from the library or save money by shopping at discount stores. The savings add up over time!

» **Ask for practical gifts!** That sweater you get from your grandmother on your birthday isn't exactly money you make, but it is potentially an opportunity for you to ask for something a little more practical from your loved ones. See if you can identify things that would make your unique situation more enjoyable and ask for them as holiday gifts. You may find that a grocery store gift cards is the best gift you get!

Wrap-up

I wanted to have real conversations with people about becoming a professional baseball player, and this is one of the more challenging conversations. Everyone's financial situation is different and it's not always clear how long a player will have to think creatively about paying their bills. But the good news is that managing your finances closely will help you develop good financial habits!

Chapter 9

PAY-TO-PLAY LEAGUES AREN'T THE
OPPORTUNITY THEY APPEAR TO BE

"Catching a fly ball is a pleasure but knowing what to do with it after you catch it is a business."

—Tommy Henrich

Sometimes, there's confusion around what "investing in yourself" really means as a professional athlete. You may hear people talk about how athletes must bet on themselves, make personal sacrifices, and even draft creative financial solutions while they work their way into professional baseball. I wanted to take this chapter to clarify which investments – financial and otherwise – you should consider.

Pay-to-Play Leagues

The most important topic I wanted to cover is pay-to-play leagues because this is where I see too many players go wrong. A pay-to-play league is appealing because it is theoretically a way to keep refining your skills. However, you may not always get what you pay for.

Any league where a player "buys in" to play on a team is what we call a "pay-to-play" league. While that isn't too hard to figure out or remember, it's important to fully understand exactly what you're buying with these leagues. For players who are at a point in their lives in which they just want to play, but they haven't received interest from any leagues, this could be an option, but for players who are still aspiring to play professional baseball, this isn't how they will meet their goal.

The requirements for pay-to-play leagues are simply too low for the player to consider the experience a professional one. Plus, when's the last time you went to work and handed your boss a stack of money so that you could come to work that day? It's just not how a job or a career ever works. While it's true that you can play in a pay-to-play league, the leagues themselves aren't professional baseball.

Other Ways to Invest in Yourself

From the first part of this chapter, you may think I discourage athletes from investing money in themselves and their professional development. That couldn't be further from the truth! All I want athletes to be sure they do is to consider all their options and what the return on their investment will be. Here are some examples of money well-spent and good decisions that may be made by an aspiring professional baseball player.

» **Coaching (Technique) –** As you focus on your professional development, you are sure to find specific areas for skill development. Whether you need to improve hitting or footwork or any other specific aspect of your game, it's hard to see what you need to do differently without an outside perspective. It's even hard sometimes for your coaches and supporters to see if they've been working with you for a long time. A professional skills coach can be a wise investment that can take you from good to great–often with just a few adjustments and tips–if you're open to the feedback and willing to do the work.

» **Coaching (Mental) –** Have you ever heard someone say something like, "Get your head in the game!" or "You need to focus!" and been left thinking, "I was focused! How am I supposed to be *more* focused?" If that sounds familiar, it's important for you to know that you aren't alone! Professional baseball players have been learning the nuances of developing your mental game for years. What's changed is the degree to which players and coaches have embraced mental training and the number of options players have now. There are a lot of skilled professionals who specialize in training athletes in their mental game.

» **Skill Training and Education –** This is a big category, and you may even lump this in with coaching, but I wanted to call attention to the diverse ways that people learn all kinds of different skills. Players read books for inspiration or practical tips, they watch videos, they attend lectures on emerging trends, and they explore other ways to grow and develop. It makes sense to add updated content to your daily routine if you're looking to develop your game. Keep an eye out for those learning opportunities!

» **Tools –** While you're exploring training and education, keep an eye out for ways to access the best new tools for measuring your performance. Advancement professionals may have access to hitting aids and throwing equipment that will help you make the most of your time and efforts. Baseball professionals are continually coming out with new ways to refine training and development, so it's critical to stay in touch with the latest developments.

» **Travel –** Athletes have access to a lot of information and resources online, and you have a lot of access to in-person resources in your town, too, but sometimes, athletes travel to play or learn, either for a short or extended period. I encourage you to search and stay open to opportunities outside your zip code. If you see an opportunity, and it doesn't work out, then it's no big deal, but if you aren't looking, then who knows what you might miss?

With all these new considerations, you might wonder how you should decide where to invest your money and your time. That's a good thing! It means you're getting the hang of taking your career as a professional baseball player seriously. If you're feeling overwhelmed, then just remember, no one runs with every idea. You must decide what is right for you.

Wrap-up

I always recommend that, in addition to talking to the player advancement professional you're working with, you talk to your most trusted advisors–the people who know you and your game the best. That is often your family and your coaches. I also encourage players to seek out professional baseball players and ask them their opinion. Your coach may know a retired player in the area or another coach a town over who could provide another perspective for you to consider. Do your research so you can make an informed decision!

Chapter 10

PROFESSIONAL BASEBALL
PLAYERS ARE MADE, NOT BORN

—◇—

"I never blame myself when I'm not hitting. I just blame the bat, and if it keeps up, I change bats."

—Yogi Berra

As a player advancement professional, I frequently talk to athletes about how their mental strength and daily habits contribute to their success. Do they also need the skills we talked about earlier in the book? Of course, they do! But the ability to continually develop skills over time is often what determines whether a player will make it to the next level.

Professional baseball players aren't born. They're developed. No matter what level of talent you start with, it takes time and focused energy to play at the professional level, so in this chapter we're going to talk about the specific steps you should consider for your own development.

89

Mental Strength

A lot of times I talk to players about what they should do—that's an empowered way to look at the future you can make for yourself. But I like the way author and mental health professional Amy Morin talks about the things mentally strong people *don't* do. In her book *13 Things Mentally Strong People Don't Do: Take Back Your Power, Embrace Change, Face Your Fears, and Train Your Brain for Happiness and Success*, she talks about a lot of things that apply to professional baseball players. I encourage you to read her entire book, but here are a few of her 13 recommendations that I felt applied to playing ball.

> » **#2 Give away their power.** *Giving away your power is a fancy way of talking about the tendency we all have to play the victim. I hear players say their parents won't pay for something they need, their coach didn't play them enough, their girlfriend doesn't support their dream, etc. We all need to vent, but if you're going to make it in a field as competitive as professional baseball, you can't afford to waste much time complaining about things you think you can't control. If your parents won't pay for something, find a way to change their mind or find a way to pay for it yourself. If your coach didn't play you enough, ask what you can do better so that you play more in the next game. If your girlfriend doesn't support you, try explaining to her how important her*

support is—or find a new girlfriend! Wherever you land, make sure you keep your power.

» **#3 Shy away from change.** *Change is hard for everyone, so I won't bother telling you how to make it easier to manage. What I will encourage you to do is recognize that change is hard and that you may need support through change. Commit to making hard decisions when they need to be made and surround yourself with the people who will keep you on track.*

» **#6 Fear taking risks.** *Baseball is a game of failure. Think about the average game and the number of times you and your teammates go to bat and don't get on base. Or think about how often you get on base, but you don't get home. The same tenacity that keeps you swinging at the plate is what you need to tap into when you're advancing your career. When you explore playing for a team, it may not work out. When you negotiate your contract, you may not get everything you want. But you better believe that if you don't take any risks, you're guaranteed not to meet your goals.*

» **#7 Dwell on the past.** *We all have embarrassing moments that we'd like to forget and things that we've experienced that make us feel angry. Carrying all of that with you will only slow you down. It's like dragging a boat anchor behind you when you're trying to get to shore. Maybe you'll still get there, but it's going to take a lot more time and effort. And it may be what keeps you from*

91

getting there at all. Letting go takes time and practice, but until you do, you're only hurting yourself.

» ***#9 Resent other people's successes.*** *When I was in college, my roommate got drafted and I didn't. That was hard at first, but eventually I realized we were both on our own paths. And as soon as I changed my thinking, some amazing things started happening. Because I wasn't wasting energy resenting the success my friend was having, I was able to see the opportunities I had in front of me. From college, I went on to play on amazing teams, develop my skills, travel the world, own a team, and eventually help other professional players realize their dreams. None of that would have happened if I had wallowed in jealousy because other people were exploring opportunities I wasn't.*

» ***#10 Give up after their first failure.*** *We already talked about how failure is a big part of baseball. Isn't it strange that so many players can go back to the plate after striking out, and yet those same players give up as soon as their first professional goal isn't met? In any highly competitive industry like baseball, you will fail more often than you succeed. You have to expect to fail often and view each failure as one of the steps needed in your development. That's what will keep you motivated.*

» ***#13 Expect immediate results.*** *Professional baseball players understand the importance of being in the game for the long haul. What you do today is unlikely to pay off today. It's unlikely to pay off tomorrow, next week, or next month. You may have a few quick wins here and there, but almost everything you do will pay off over time. The important decision you need to make is to be patient and wait for that payoff and, when you're experiencing positive results, to look back and acknowledge the work you did previously that got you to where you are.*

I hope you check out the complete list because all 13 suggestions that Morin makes are valuable. These are just the ones that really stood out to me. So many players waste time on fear, anger, and jealousy. It's worth investing in your own mental strength and learning how to spot the most common pitfalls from a distance.

Forming Habits

All the things mentioned in this book are supported by good habits, so the last half of this chapter will be devoted to discussing the best practices I've developed over the years to create and maintain good habits. A lot of my inspiration comes from *The Compound Effect* by Darren Hardy, and I encourage you to read that, too, as you look for ways to improve your skills.

One thing I talk to my players about all the time comes straight from *The Compound Effect*. The slight changes that you make in your life consistently add up to huge rewards. Not hitting snooze every morning adds hours to your week. Showing up early to every practice with your head in the game boosts your confidence and speeds your progress.

Another important lesson I learned and often share from that book is the importance of taking responsibility for your own success and happiness. If you don't like something about your life, you are the person most able to make the changes needed to alter your environment. To some people, that may feel overwhelming. They may think that being able to blame others and cite reasons why they can't be successful helps them and makes them feel better, but it won't move you forward.

Finally, another piece of mental strength that I like to recommend is the importance of gratitude. If you spend every day angry about the opportunities you weren't given, the homeruns you didn't hit, or the rejections you've experienced, then you'll feel discouraged, and your progress will stagnate, but if you go through each day acknowledging and appreciating the opportunities you've been given, then you will feel energized. Your strength to persevere comes from within, so remember to take care of yourself with thankful thinking.

Wrap-up

Mental strength and a commitment to good habits is what gets the professional baseball player where they want to be. We were all born with different skills and talents, and it may seem like some people have an easier path to professional ball than others. But no one gets there solely on luck and no one stays there without waking up every day with a renewed commitment to the game.

Chapter 11

YOU CAN'T PLAY
BASEBALL FOREVER!

"I knew when my career was over.
In 1965 my baseball card came out with no picture."

—Bob Uecker

This is an area I'm sure you understand on some level, but it's important and a little hard to accept sometimes, so I wanted to devote a chapter of this book to the topic. It is extremely unlikely that playing professional baseball will be your first and last career. I'm not saying you can't play pro ball your entire life or that you can't have a career in baseball. And I do want you to stay focused right now on what you need to do to play professionally. But it's also a good idea to think about what you may love to do after you retire from playing.

Why can't we play forever?

We grow up idolizing talented players – typically, the ones who have lengthy careers with a lot of highlights. It's certainly possible that you'll be one of those talented players, but it's more likely that if you stay committed to the game and make it to a professional league, then you'll end up retiring relatively early in your life. If you're 20 years old and reading this, then retiring from baseball in your 30s – or even 40s – may not sound that young, but it is! Most people in other careers work for decades after that!

It's also important to remember that, unlike other careers, you may be injured at some point, and that injury could bring your professional baseball career to an unplanned pause – or even a premature end. We never know what may happen, so it's important to have a back-up plan (or two).

Careers in Baseball

There are a lot of things that can bring your career in baseball to an end: an injury, a more talented player, or simply the end of your contract. For some players, this transition is devastating and paralyzing because they can't imagine leaving the game, and they have no idea what to do next.

There are a lot of different ways that you can stay connected to the game once your career as a player has ended. I've listed some ideas below, but this certainly isn't every possibility! I encourage you to stay open to even more ideas to combine your love of the game with opportunities that come your way.

>> **Coaching –** Coaching is a logical progression from playing, and there are a lot of different areas you can coach. Not everyone has the skills to meaningfully connect with players and give them feedback to improve their game, but if you do, then this could be an amazing way to contribute to the game long-term – and you wouldn't have to coach in the MLB! There are coaching opportunities at every level, so keep your options open if this is an area that interests you.

>> **Scouts –** Like coaching, not everyone has an eye for talent, but if the "big picture" of a team interests you and you find that you have an ability to spot skills that can build a team, scouting may be an area you'd like to explore.

>> **Team Leadership –** Owning a team is an investment that isn't an option for everyone, but maybe it's an option for you? If not, there are still ways to lead a team by working with the team owner as a manager or other front office employee. Remember that baseball is a business, so if you have skills that align with business and management, you may be able to

apply them to the game through this kind of role.

» **Sportswriter** – Did you excel in your writing classes in college? There are all kinds of ways to write for baseball players and fans. You may find an opportunity in anything from writing a regular column to supporting a marketing team with written content. Knowing the lingo and understanding the game gives you a big advantage over other writers!

» **Analyst** – If you have an interest in math and statistics, there are jobs that combine that skill with the game of baseball! Color commentators, sports writers, trainers, team owners, and others all use stats to report and make decisions. If you're interested in gathering, creating, and interpreting data, this could be a great option.

» **Leadership** – Committed athletes share a lot of traits with leaders in a variety of organizations. If you look at top CEOs, you'll find an amazingly high percentage of them were involved in organized sports at some point in their lives. That's because the mental techniques that you need to be successful in business are also what you need to be successful as a leader outside of sports. Whether you retire from baseball to work for a family business, pursue a career in what you studied in college, or land in a completely new industry, professional baseball will have set you up to be successful.

I loved playing baseball, and through most of my early years, I dreamed of playing in the big leagues, just like every other aspiring player. As I grew older, my commitment to the game remained strong, and I realized that I still loved playing baseball, but it was more accurate to say that I loved the game. Eventually, I realized there were a lot of different ways that I could be a part of the game, so I began to explore them all. My advice is to focus on playing for as long as you can but keep an open mind about your future.

Careers Outside Baseball

There is, of course, the option of a career outside baseball once you leave the game! A lot of professional players are fortunate enough to find a second passion in life that they can pick up once they retire from the game. What interested you in college? When you worked in the offseason, what kind of work were you good at? Answering some of these questions can be a great way to create a plan for yourself after baseball, and remember, the work you put into your professional baseball career will help you in any other career you pick up.

Wrap-up

I hope this chapter has given you some ideas for how you can keep working in the game you love — even after your role as a player has ended. Enjoy playing for as long as you can but remember not to close any doors or burn any bridges along the way. You never know what opportunities will find you if you stay open to them!

Chapter 12

FAILURE AND
SUCCESS ARE THE SAME

―――――――∞――――――――

"Every day is a new opportunity. You can build on yesterday's success or put its failures behind and start over again. That's the way life is, with a new game every day, and that's the way baseball is."

—Bob Feller

When you started playing baseball, you probably figured out quickly that it's a game of failure. When you think about all your at-bats, how often did you end up on base, and for every time you ended up on base, how many times did you get home? When you executed a play as an outfielder or infielder, how often did you succeed?

The percentage of at-bats and plays that aren't successful are high – and that's to be expected! You're playing against the top athletes from around the world. When top players come together in competition, the fact that they are so well matched is exactly why all players fail so frequently.

But those failures don't just happen on the field; they're part of your development and your goals. There's an old story about a CEO who was interviewing a potential new leader for their organization. When asked about their greatest accomplishment, the interviewee said, "I've never failed. Every project I've ever taken on, I've completed successfully." The CEO smiled and said that was a great example because it told him exactly what he needed to know — that the candidate wasn't a fit for his organization.

The candidate was stunned, of course. He thought he had shared an impressive statistic that would be sure to land him the job, but what he didn't realize was that by telling the CEO he had never failed, he was also telling the CEO he always played it safe. He never stretched his ambitions. This candidate wasn't going to take the organization to the next level because this candidate was content to be average.

That's why I tell players that failure and success are two sides of the same coin. You can't have one without the other. Plus, all the failures you experience will make your success that much more amazing!

Wrap-up

You made it to the end of the book! I hope now you feel like you know a little more about playing professional baseball and, even more than that, I hope you have a plan for making your dream of playing professional baseball a reality!

Chapter 13

DIVISIONS IN
SCOUTING DEPARTMENTS

❯❮❯❮❯

"I'm not an athlete; I'm a baseball player."

—John Kruk

S ince you're looking to catch the attention of scouts, it helps to understand where scouts are coming from, what they may be thinking, and what all the language they use means. In this chapter, we'll start with a little history, and then unravel the mystery of professional baseball scouts.

The Beginning

Professional scouting practices have been used for more than 100 years in various forms, and they are still evolving today. Early on, club owners realized there was a lot of value in finding the best talent and recruiting them to their team, so they invested in the process.

20-80 Scale

Scouts use what's called the "20-80 Scale" to consistently compare and discuss player skills. On the scale, 20-30 is well below average, 40 is below average, 50 is average, 60 is above average, and 70-80 is well above average. Although these grades are subjective based on the scout that reports them, having one scale allows scouts to communicate with each other and their bosses easier and more accurately.

Scouting Departments

Within organizations, scouts focus on different areas. Depending on need and the time of year, there may be some shifting or even overlap in the work they do, but typically there is a pro, amateur, and international department who operate independent of one another.

No matter who may be scouting you, you're going to show up the same way every day — by giving 100% — but when players don't understand the game, or the variety of scouts who may approach them, it can lead to missed opportunities. For example, you may not know that there aren't any Minor League scouts. Major League scouts look for talent, draft them, and assign them to their Minor League affiliate.

What are scouts looking at?

If a scout comes to see you, then they are coming to measure your performance based on the statistics they've already read about your game, and the video footage they've already watched. It's exciting to reach that next step — and a fitting example of why every game matters — but it's also important to understand that scouts start with your performance data before they meet you. The meeting is so that they can confirm what kind of player you are.

Scouts will be interested in seeing where your head is. No matter which of your skills interested them, they're considering you for a *team*. They need to see what your understanding of the game is, what your maturity level is, and how much you understand professional baseball. No one expects perfection, but a scout is going to be more interested in a player who can smoothly join a team because they have developed people skills; they know how to get along well with others, and they have a good head on their shoulders.

Wrap-up

Professional baseball players need to understand how important scouts are and what their role is in baseball because it's an important one. Understanding what questions to ask and what opportunity each scout could offer you is critical to your success.

SECTION IV

WHAT YOU NEED TO KNOW
(AND WHY)

"Whenever we had career day at elementary school, and we could dress up like what you wanted to be, when I got on stage, mine was playing major league baseball."

—Jacob deGrom

I wish I could say that all you need is talent or commitment to the game to make it as a professional baseball player. That would make life so much easier! But that isn't reality. You need talent, commitment to the game, and business sense.

In the following chapters, I'm going to share a few insights into making it as a professional baseball player that may sound a little discouraging. There are opportunities that seem like everything you've been looking for and I'm going to tell you why they're a bad idea. There are paths to playing professionally that you thought weren't for real players and I'm going to tell you why they may be your best option. My goal for this section of the book is for you to know what questions to ask when opportunities present themselves and for you believe me when I say every opportunity that comes your way may not be what it seems.

Chapter 14

WHAT COULD
POSSIBLY GO WRONG?

—◇—

"People do think that if they avoid the truth, it might change to something better before they have to hear it."

—Marsha Norman

Have you ever wanted something so badly that you ignored all the signs telling you it was a bad idea? For example, the first time you bought a car, and you finally found one you could afford, it was so exciting that you ignored the terrible shape the car was in, and how it needed more maintenance than you could keep up with. A lot of us can name situations in which people (sometimes ourselves) made bad choices — despite all the evidence telling them not to!

Why is this so common, and what can we learn from it when we consider our professional baseball careers?

I'm sorry to say that many aspiring professional baseball players hear about opportunities to play and, despite having information at their fingertips that would encourage them not to, they end up making the wrong choices for their professional careers. In this chapter, I'm going to share some of the mistakes I've seen and even made myself, as well as what you can do to avoid the same or similar pitfalls.

Facts vs. Opinions

Let's start by looking at some facts that we know are true.

> » **Major League Baseball contracts 42 teams.**
> » **A lot more players are trying to make those teams than there are spots on the roster.**

» **The pandemic that began in 2020 changed baseball – there were short-term changes and changes made that will last.**

What are opinions that you might here? Someone may tell you they have the perfect opportunity for you. Someone may tell you that giving them money is your surest way to play professional baseball. There are all kinds of things people may say that we want to accept as a fact because, if it were a fact, it would make your dream that much closer to being a reality. And the fact that we want so badly to believe opinions that, if they are accurate, will make our lives better, is what makes them so dangerous.

The Florida Winter Baseball League

The Florida Winter Baseball League (FWBL) was a professional baseball league that started and ended in 2009. I wanted to write about the FWBL because I had personal experience with that league. It looked like a fantastic opportunity to me, so I became involved, but I also paid attention; I was careful, and I asked tough questions. It's still a difficult professional memory for me because to most people, the league only looks like a failure, but for me, it was a valuable lesson, which is why I want to share the story with you.

The FWBL had four teams and had planned a 60-game schedule. As the name suggests, the games were scheduled through winter in multiple markets in Florida. But after only

15 of the scheduled games, it was discovered that the organization didn't have the startup capital it needed to continue.

I was embarrassed because I was associated with a league that popped up and then disappeared so quickly. I wasn't financing the league, but I was still working with it and had colleagues that were associated with it. I did help people understand that the league was having challenges, and I did help different people recover after the league was shut down. But I also had to ask myself if there was anything I missed early on. Were there other questions I should have asked?

Wrap-up

Even though I have decades of experience, I am still careful not to get caught up in the myths and scams we talked about in the previous section. I still remind myself to ask tough questions if something seems too good to be true.

As you continue to read this section, pay attention to all the ways you can play professional baseball and make note of the questions you should ask!

Chapter 15

LEAGUES, DIVISIONS, AND CLASSIFICATIONS

"It's the same game. It's baseball. National League, American League. It's baseball. I just come here and try to do my thing. Do my work and help the team to win."

—Asdrubal Cabrera

Professional baseball players are often most interested in MLB affiliates. You'll hear them called "Minor League" or "farm" teams, but everyone knows they are connected to a Major League Baseball team, so joining one is taking one step closer to the big leagues.

There are two leagues in the MLB – the American League and the National League. Within each league, there are three divisions – East, West, and Central. And then, of course, within each division, there are teams.

Leagues are divided into six classes:

» **AAA**
» **AA**
» **A**
» **Low A**
» **Class A Short Season**
» **Rookie**

Triple-A and Double-A leagues typically have more experienced players whereas A and Rookie leagues usually younger, less experienced players. Ideally, players "move up the ladder" as they progress from lower levels toward the Major Leagues. Players can be called up to the MLB from any level at any time, but most players spend several years in the minors honing their skills. That's why so many are in AA or AAA classes when they move to the big leagues.

Wrap-up

There are a lot of leagues and classifications to consider, but there still aren't that many spots on affiliate teams. If your plan is to be drafted to one of these teams right out of school, you better have a back-up. This is the most talked about path and it might be the path for you, but we're going to talk about your other options, too!

Chapter 16

THE DRAFT

"You realize it's a business and that teams are going to do what's best for them. That's how it is. That's what we sign up for as a Major League Baseball player."

—Christian Yelich

No matter the level in which you play professional baseball, it's important that you at least understand the draft. The MLB First-Year Player Draft involves all Major League Clubs taking turns selecting players. Selection order is the reverse of their won-lost records from the previous season.

Who's eligible for the draft?

A popular and logical first question a lot of people ask is, "Who's eligible for the draft?" Over time, rules have changed and I'm sure they will continue to evolve, but as it stands today, here are the general eligibility guidelines.

» Residents of the United States or Canada who have never signed a Major League or Minor League contract

» Residents of U.S. territories (like Puerto Rico)

» Players who enroll in high school or college in the United States

» High school players (if they graduate high school and do not attend college)

» College players at four-year institutions who are at least 21 years old and have completed their junior year

» Junior college players

If a player isn't drafted, they become a free agent which I share more about in the next chapter.

What happens after the draft?

Players who are planning their careers in professional baseball often get really focused on the draft, but it's important to think about what follows the draft, too. While staying on top of your game, it's also important for to pay attention to how the business of baseball may affect your career. Here are some additional details about what happens after a player is drafted.

1. A player is **bound to the team that drafts them for three seasons,** and then contracts are renewed one year at a time. At the three-year mark, a player must be on the

40-man roster, or they are eligible for the Rule 5 draft.

2. At that time, **a player can be drafted by another team** for $50,000 but there is a risk for the drafting team. The drafting team must keep that player on the 25-man major-league roster for the entire next season or the original team can bring them back for $25,000.

3. If a player is **not on the 40-man roster and not taken in the Rule 5 draft**, they are still under contract with their current organization. They can choose to become a minor-league free agent instead of being taken in the Rule 5 draft, but players rarely do so.

4. After six years of MLB service time, a professional player is eligible to become a **free agent**.

5. Within their six years, an organization may **release a player**, making them a free agent.

Wrap-up

The history of free agency is important for you to know and understand. As a free agent, a player is free to sign with any club, but that wasn't always an option. Many professionals in baseball had to work to make that change happen and many other changes are happening that continue to make the game better for all of us.

Chapter 17

FREE AGENTS

———————— ◦⟨◇⟩◦ ————————

"Just because you go to free agency doesn't mean you don't want to be somewhere. It's just a part of the business."

—Mookie Betts

Managing a career as a free agent is a reality a lot of professional baseball players. At what point in their career and for how long varies, of course, but it is common enough that those shaping their baseball career need to understand what is involved.

I'll start with a little history, and a few facts about what working as a free agent is and isn't. In keeping with the theme of this book, I want to be clear that every professional baseball player's journey is different, and no one will be given the same series of opportunities. Understanding that your path may look different than your teammate's — and accepting that "different" doesn't mean "bad" — is the key to maintaining your motivation and solid decision-making.

The History of Free Agency

If you know baseball history, you've probably heard of Curt Flood. His case, brought to the Supreme Court in the 1970's, started the conversations that would eventually end what was called the reserve clause. As a result of Flood's case, the MLB conceded and gave players a broader range of options as free agents.

The relationship between Major League Baseball and its players continues to evolve. Prior to 2011, free agents were either Type A, Type B, or unclassified, depending on their ranking from the previous season. Beginning with the 2012 season, players are no longer classified by type. If they have six or more years on a Major League Baseball 40-man roster and are not under contract for the next season, they are automatically a free agent.

These changes may seem slow, and your opportunities may seem to come and go quickly but keeping up with what free agency is, and how it is evolving, is worth your time. There is a business side to baseball that isn't as enjoyable as playing for most of us, but it is important for our professional and personal success.

Just Keep Playing

If you aren't drafted, you can still have a career as a professional baseball player on an Independent team. You can play overseas, or you can sign as a free agent. Before I played professional baseball, I remember thinking that I'd go from college to an MLB affiliate. That wasn't the exact path my career took, and I was so distracted by what I thought was supposed to happen that I almost missed my opportunity to play professional baseball when other professional organizations expressed an interest. One of my goals as a player advancement professional is to make sure no other player makes the same mistake I almost did. In any professional sport, you need to keep playing to advance your career, and sometimes that means being open to alternative career paths.

Understanding what it means to be a free agent is the first step in preparing yourself for the opportunities that may come your way. You may never work as a free agent, but if you understand the details, you'll be best prepared to decide if it's the right choice for you.

In It for the Long Haul

You may be a free agent right out of high school or college, or you may play on a professional team and then become a free agent. It's even possible that, while playing for a team, you may reach an agreement with management that you can solicit offers from other teams as a free agent. The point is that being a free agent doesn't have a single definition or timeframe for professional baseball players. It's a possibility for your entire career.

Jack Morris is the perfect example of a pitcher who just kept going. After a lengthy career with the Detroit Tigers, he left the team at age 35 after a career-high number of losses. Not one to go out on a low note, he signed a one-year contract with the Minnesota Twins. In that one year, he went on to win a World Series Championship and was named the World Series MVP. Morris continued to play on other teams and eventually retired, leaving professional baseball players with a fitting example of how our perception of a player's career can change from one contract to the next.

How Alone Are Free Agents?

When I talk to players about the times when they were playing without a contract and without an agent, they often acknowledge that they were on their own – making their own decisions and doing the best they could do with the information they had. It's a daunting idea to consider negotiating a contract for the first time on your own when the people you're negotiating with have years of experience. But the good news is that if you really explore each player's situations, they're rarely completely alone. Within the baseball community, there are all kinds of people supporting players coming up through the ranks – and that support may come from surprising places.

Nick Singleton, whose professional success included a decade of pitching for International and Independent Leagues, recalled how important his network was when it came to signing contracts. He tells the story of being recruited to play for a team in Mexico by a former teammate who spoke fluent English and Spanish. Not only did his former teammate recommend him for the team; he also translated contract negotiations for him and ended up being his roommate when they were on the road. Nick was a talented player, but a big part of the reason opportunity presented itself to him was because he was also a great person, a team player, and an active part of the baseball community.

There are more formal — though often short-term — supporters who help players with the business side of baseball. Brokers, for example, can often be hired and paid a percentage of a contract, as needed. As a player advancement professional, one of the things I try to do is help players navigate all the people, tools, and resources available. However, as in Nick's case, a good reputation is often the greatest asset you can cultivate.

Part of Baseball History

Free agents are an important part of baseball today and an important part of the history of baseball. When the concept was new, owners worried that all players would want to become free agents every year! If they were right, this would of course be too much to manage. The compromise they agreed on was that players could only become free agents if their contract had expired, and they had at least six years in the major leagues. It worked out well for players, too. Since only a portion of players become free agents at any given point in time, the market is much more favorable for their negotiations.

Wrap-up

After considering all the details associated with being a free agent, what do you really need to know? Here are a few things I'd like you to remember.

>> Just because you aren't drafted on the timeline and in the way that you were expecting, **doesn't mean you can't work as a professional baseball player**. I want you to think about the other leagues, but I also want you to think about what it might mean to be a free agent.

>> There are a lot of considerations associated with being a free agent and **I don't recommend managing those considerations on your own**. If you do find yourself operating as a free agent, make sure you have the right support network in place to help you make the right decisions – and those decisions extend past career moves. Your support network also helps you stay motivated and working hard to fulfill your dreams.

» You may **become a free agent at various points in your career**. In fact, you may be a free agent, get drafted, and end up working as a free agent again! Part of a professional baseball career involves managing those changes.

Chapter 18

THE INDEPENDENT LEAGUES

"The difference between the impossible and the possible lies in a man's determination."

—Tommy Lasorda

Independent Baseball Leagues are professional baseball organizations in the United States and Canada that have no ties to the MLB or any Minor League team. They benefit from not being affiliated, but some people don't realize that these leagues still attract professional players. In this chapter, we're going to learn a little more about the Independent Leagues, and why you should consider them when mapping out your professional baseball career.

Let's start by looking at the Independent Leagues that have been around for a while. Keep in mind that this isn't every league, just a few that you may want to check out if you're interested in learning more about Independent Leagues in general.

> » **The Frontier League** was started in 1993 and covers the Midwest, Western Pennsylvania, Northeast, Quebec
> » **The Atlantic League of Professional Baseball** played their first game in 1998. They're in the Northeast and Greater Houston area. It's worth noting that more marquee players like Jose Canseco and Carlos Baerga have come out of this league than any other Independent League.
> » **The American Association of Independent Professional Baseball** was started in 2006 and plays in the Midwest, Texas, and Manitoba.

Fortunately for professional baseball players, Independent Leagues have been growing and changing for decades. Thanks to the Independent Leagues, thousands of players have had the opportunity to successfully pursue their dream of playing ball. The Independent Leagues have changed over time, so I'm going to reference the ones that have been around the longest. You may know about other leagues that I don't mention, but don't let that worry you. Just because I don't mention them doesn't mean they aren't a good option for you. Like always, do your research and let what I share here contribute to your decision.

Playing in an Independent League

The Independent League environment is fast paced. What a lot of people don't realize is that players feel the pressure to win every day because if they don't, they may get sent home. Some rookies don't make it through two weeks, and not everyone can handle that kind of pressure.

I've known players who wouldn't even unpack – at first, because they were sure they were going to get cut, and then because they thought that not unpacking was good luck! It's a reality that all professional baseball players live with, but the feeling of earning your place every day is strongest in the Independent Leagues. If you can manage the stress there, then you can handle anything.

Wrap-up

The baseball community is fortunate to have the Independent Leagues, and they may be the perfect place for you to play. They are competitive; don't think that if you don't get drafted, you can "just play in an Independent League". You will compete against top players, and you will have to work hard to stay relevant.

Chapter 19

THE INTERNATIONAL LEAGUES

---

*"There is no room in baseball for discrimination.
It is our national pastime and a game for all."*

—Lou Gehrig

With the work that I do now, I try to help athletes avoid the mistakes I made and grab the opportunities I missed. Of course, along the way, I did some things right, too! And working in baseball overseas is one thing I count without any hesitation as a good decision I made. For me, the opportunity came up to work with an international team when I was hoping to get recruited by an MLB team.

Getting Signed

A common and smart initial question I hear from players thinking about playing overseas is, "So, how do I get signed by an overseas team?" It doesn't take too long for anyone to realize things are probably a little different from the start.

As a player advancement professional, I connect professional baseball players with teams all around the world, based on the player's goals and the team's needs. Sometimes, I can help with introductions, or I'm more directly involved with players, weighing options, and securing contracts.

There are also organizations like Baseball Jobs Overseas where players can actively seek out opportunities outside of their home country. David Burns, founder of Baseball Jobs Overseas, created the organization when he realized there was an opportunity for players like himself to follow a less traditional path to playing baseball for a living. His own story is the perfect example of how a committed player with a carefully managed reputation can find new opportunities to keep playing.

"I decided to forego a college baseball career. Growing up where I did in Canada, at the time, there [weren't] really college baseball opportunities. I decided to not play college baseball and just study locally, and then just continued to play in a men's league there – even though I feel like I maybe had the talent to go do something – and then in between my sophomore and junior year[s], I got a phone call from a buddy [who] was playing in Austria. He called me up and said, "Hey, do you wanna hop on a plane and come over and play for a couple months this summer?" So, I jumped on that and went over to Austria and long story short, that was in 1999, and so 21 years later, here I am, still in Austria. I did return to Canada for about four years, and then moved here permanently. I have two kids here, who are now almost adults, and I continued to play baseball this whole time in Austria – even today, I'm still up there, swinging the bat."

Burns didn't even realize that his decision to stay open to all the different ways he could play professional baseball would lead to him founding an organization that continues to help players to do the same, but two decades later, Baseball Job Overseas is still going strong. And it's safe to assume that the organization is so successful because the opportunities for players to find just the right fit are so valuable.

Who are international teams looking to sign?

Determining what teams look for in international players isn't much different than determining what local teams are looking for – with one possible exception. If a team is going to bring you onboard from a different country, you must be a significantly better player than those they have access to in their own region. They must need your specific skills, and you must shine brighter than any of the other options they may be looking at.

However, there is another level to consider if you're thinking about playing outside your home country. Players obviously live where they work; therefore, you must be the kind of person who's excited by – not just "willing to accept" – the prospect of living in a different country. A lot of considerations often come with that: different weather, different food, not having access to the stores you're used to. No one wants to leave their favorite restaurant behind, right? If you think about that and cringe, then playing baseball outside your own country may not be the way to nurture your talent. You may find that you're simply too distracted by the differences. However, if the new surroundings sound exciting – or at least intriguing – then it could be a good fit.

I asked David Burns what he thinks are the most important traits of successful International Baseball players, and he shared similar sentiments.

"The ultimate import from the standpoint of a club overseas is not only somebody that would come over and be a dominant player in whatever league that may be, but also somebody [who] is like an ambassador of the game, who is eager to share their knowledge and to help grow the game internationally, from the youth program that club may have all the way up to their teammates, helping them improve [the] players themselves. So, the ultimate guy has a very strong character, is a little bit worldly or interested in learning about other cultures and whatnot, as well, and is also a good player."

That sums it up, doesn't it? You must be a talented player, of course, but you also must want to see and live in unfamiliar places around the world. When baseball is your career, it affects every aspect of your life, and when you choose to pursue International Baseball connections, you must make sure you're looking at the full range of what those choices could mean for you.

Wrap-up

Sometimes, I hear players say that if they don't make the draft, they'll just "go play on a team overseas somewhere". While that may be a great next step, I always worry a bit when those comments are made with too much certainty. There are teams around the world that perform at extremely important levels, and most importantly, there are players around the world who are working just as hard to play professional baseball. International teams aren't where professional players can "just go if they don't make the draft"; they're an option that professional players can work toward if they choose.

Chapter 20

SALARIES, SEASONS, AND TRAVEL

"*Travel isn't always pretty. It isn't always comfortable. Sometimes it hurts, it even breaks your heart. But that's okay. The journey changes you; it should change you. It leaves marks on your memory, on your consciousness, on your heart, and on your body. You take something with you. Hopefully, you leave something good behind.*"

—Anthony Bourdain

While a lot of what players ask about related to playing baseball internationally results in the same advice as what I say to anyone interested in playing professionally, there are a few unique considerations. In this chapter, I've recapped what's the same, but I've also shared thoughts on some of the questions I hear most often.

Before you dig into the details, I want to offer a little more advice about considering playing baseball outside of the country you are familiar with. I understand that living and working in a new country – especially if you don't know the language and do know that there are significant cultural differences – can be a little intimidating. But if you can find a way to manage those concerns, you may have the opportunity to embark on one of the greatest experiences you'll have in your life. I know that my time playing outside the United States helped me be a better player and leverage myself professionally, but I also grew as a person. I developed a new understanding of people and of what it means to be on a team.

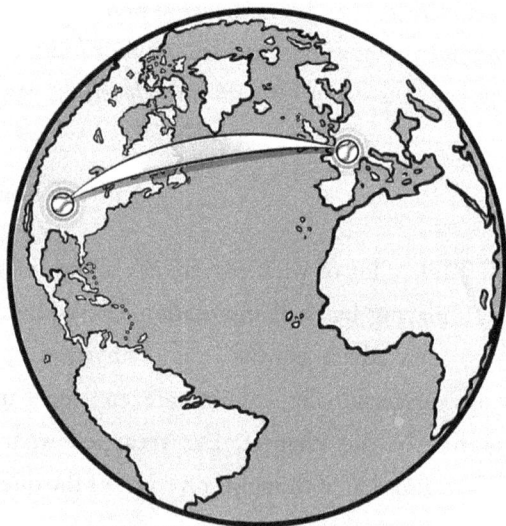

What's the same about International Baseball?

There are a lot of similarities between baseball at a professional level outside the U.S. and what you already know about playing baseball for a team based in the United States.

> » **It's still competitive.** If you think you'll just pick an international team to join if nothing in the U.S. works out, then you need to think again. Just like teams in the U.S., teams around the world are looking for top talent. In fact, as I'll talk about later in this chapter, you may find that you're held to an even higher performance standard if you're recruited from a different country, so be prepared to work hard to earn and keep your spot on the team.

> » **It's still a job.** You aren't playing on an international team to stay warm and wait for a bigger break. You have a coach and a team that expect you to show up and perform your best every day. You also represent the team on and off the field and that means you'll likely have rules you'll need to learn and follow.

> » **It can still open doors for your long-term plans as a professional ballplayer.** As it becomes easier for the entire world to stay connected through video, phone calls, air travel, and all things digital, recruiters have learned how to leverage these tools to recruit

around the globe. If you're an onion – that is, the player that another team really needs – then taking advantage of these tools is a wonderful way to land future opportunities.

As many similarities as there are, there are also some significant differences, so the rest of this chapter is dedicated to explaining those differences, so you can be prepared for them. Here are some of the most frequently asked questions about International Baseball.

Can you play International Baseball as a steppingstone to the MLB?

To provide additional insight into this question, I ran it past David Burns of Baseball Jobs Overseas. Here's what David had to say.

"It usually breaks down to two types of individuals that are looking to play overseas. There's the guy that's looking to extend his career and see some of the world and there's the guy that still has the MLB dream. We try to differentiate between them and then we give them different advice. We try to be as real as possible to the guy with the MLB dream that if you're looking overseas then the MLB dream is pretty much over."

David and I are on the same page here – anything is possible, but the biggest benefit of playing overseas is simply the opportunity to play. Showing up every day as an amazing player may get you noticed by other teams, but even if it

146

doesn't, you're still enjoying life as a professional baseball player.

Should I play in a country if I don't speak the language?

A common and understandable question that I often hear is whether an athlete can be successful playing in a country where they don't speak the language. How do you get around if you can't read the signs? How do you buy things you need if you can't talk to people? It may seem impossible, so I always share a few considerations that a lot of players don't realize.

> » **You'll have a lot of support from your team.** Remember that your journey outside of your own country is happening because you're joining a team. There will be people assigned to help you get settled and acclimated to your environment and it won't be long before you make friends on your team as well.

> » **English translations are more common than you'd think.** If you've never traveled outside the United States, then you'll be surprised to see just how much English there is in the rest of the world! Often, transportation hubs (e.g., airports, train stations, etc.) and stores will have enough English translations available for you to navigate on your own with little difficulty. You'll also develop a whole new appreciation

for pictures! There are a lot of universal images (e.g., restrooms, stairways, transportation, etc.) that will help you find your way.

» **Pocket translators are more affordable and more accurate than you'd think.** If you invest a few hundred dollars in a pocket translator, you'll also be able to ask simple questions as needed and translate longer written text if you need additional details. It's a simple tool that is surprisingly accurate and can make your life a lot easier!

» **Learning the language will help you make connections.** It's important not to interpret the previous points as advice on how to get by only speaking English. You should attempt to learn the language of the country you're living in! You don't have to be fluent, and the previous ideas will help you as needed, but if you try to learn the language, people will appreciate your efforts. That alone will make them more willing to connect with and help you.

Will I be treated differently if people know I'm from the United States?

Depending on the country you play in, you may stand out quite a bit. If, for example, you're 6' 2" with blonde hair and you're playing in a country where the population is primarily Asian, it's safe to assume you're going to stand out in a crowd. Typically, that isn't an issue, but it is a good idea to mentally prepare yourself for the experience!

On your team, you may be treated differently, as well, but in a unique way. If you've been recruited from another country, then it's likely that your teammates will wonder why. Since their leadership has gone so far to bring you onboard, they'll expect you to bring something amazing to the game. It's natural for them to hold you to a higher standard — or even scrutinize what you do. Like standing out in a crowd in the grocery store, the best thing you can do is be prepared for their potential response. The next-best thing you can do is use that preparation to always respond respectfully to their questions. Taking the bait or picking a fight will only leave you farther behind as you work to become part of the team.

Are there different rules in different countries?

While a lot of the game and the skills you need to be successful will be the same, it is possible that from country to country, there will be slight differences, but you've already learned how to make the adjustments you need to be successful when you play in different ballparks, with a full crowd or empty bleachers, or after a long bus ride. Part of being a professional baseball player means making the needed adjustments to be successful.

It's also important to remember that, just like navigating a country where you don't speak the language, you're not doing this alone. The recruiter, coach, and your teammates have a personal stake in your success. If you show up with the right attitude, then you'll make any needed adjustments without issue.

What will I do in my downtime?

Being a professional baseball player requires an intense commitment level. Wherever you play, your life will revolve around your game. But you will still develop friendships, go out to dinner, and visit tourist attractions! Again, your team will be a great connection for how you'll enjoy the country you're playing in, but you will also find your own groove and learn how to explore your own genuine interests.

What kind of salary can I expect?

Again, the salaries will vary according to the league you're working with, so it is an important question to ask while you're doing your research about various teams around the world. You should plan for a small stipend that you'll need to supplement, but it's possible that you will land on an international team that pays you well enough to comfortably cover all your expenses.

There are a few important questions people sometimes forget to ask when they're mapping out their finances, so I've listed them below.

> » **What is the cost of living in the country?** You're probably familiar with the concept of cost of living, but you may not realize how extreme the differences can be from one country to the next. Make sure that you not only understand what your salary will be, but how much you will need to cover your basic expenses.

> » **How long are the seasons?** With so many different opportunities and leagues, you may be surprised to learn how many different calendars there are. When you're talking about a commitment to play, be sure to clarify when you'll be playing and for how long. This can help you determine how much money you need

to earn in the off-season and how much time you'll have to earn it.

» **What will be covered or supported by the team?** It's best to assume that you will be responsible for all your expenses, but your teammates or coaches might help you find ways to pay for some of your necessities. For example, you may have the opportunity to share housing, or they might offer ideas for the best places to buy food.

» **What will it cost to travel home to the United States, and how often will I be allowed to go?** One of the hardest parts for professional athletes who play internationally is being so far from friends and family, who are such an important part of their lives. It's important to recognize that your commitment to playing professional baseball will make seeing loved ones challenging sometimes. Research the cost of airline tickets and think about how comfortable you'll feel missing birthdays and holidays before making your commitment, but also remember that no matter where you play as a professional, you will have to sacrifice some of the friend-and-family time you love. It's one of the hardest parts of being an athlete.

What's the best way to learn about what it's really like to play on an international team?

Finally, my last piece of advice for anyone thinking about playing baseball outside the United States is to ask someone who's already done it! Ideally, you can find someone who's played on the specific team you're considering, but even if that's not an option, you can learn a lot from anyone who has made a career for themselves playing International Baseball. Most players are happy to share their experiences – even the mistakes they've made! Try asking them some of the questions from this chapter, or any of the questions on your mind. Baseball is a strong community, and you'll be pleasantly surprised by the number of people who are happy to help you.

Wrap-up

As a player advancement professional and former professional International Baseball player, I can attest to the number of people who are willing to make the connections you need to get your questions answered. If the player you're talking to doesn't have the answer you need, then they probably know someone who does. It's up to you to start the conversation!

Chapter 21

TAKING ACTION

―――――――――⌒✕⌒―――――――――

"Vision without action is merely a dream. Action without vision just passes the time. Vision with action can change the world."

—Joel A. Barker

Now that you've come to the end of the book, you can see the big picture. You know what it takes to be a professional baseball player, so it's time to prepare for the unique opportunities that may come to you. Here's how to do that.

1. **Consider each chapter of this book and make a list**. What areas do you need to change to be successful? For example, learning more about motivation or working with a professional to improve a part of your game. As you review what you've read, make a quick note of

anything that stands out as an opportunity for you.

2. Now that you have your list of opportunities, **put them into action**. For each opportunity, list what you need to do to bring what you need into your life. Continuing with the previous example, you might read a book to learn more about motivation, so the steps you may take could be research. Or you may want to hire a professional to help you with a specific skill, so you'd need to do research and figure out how you'll pay to hire someone. Everyone who reads this book will have a unique list of opportunities and each opportunity will have a unique plan.

3. As you make decisions, **check your understanding and your bias**. That is easier than you think – it just means asking the tough questions. Does the person offering you advice have anything to gain? Does the opportunity you're considering align with what you've learned about professional baseball? How long has the person offering you a great opportunity been in business? Whether they are an agent or an ownership group, how established are they? That's important because their experience shows that they've been through some things.

Becoming a professional baseball player is an exciting journey, but you won't get there without making a plan and putting in the work. Playing professionally is a commitment to a lifestyle.

Thank You for reading GETTING PAID TO PLAY. I hope you found the information to be a valuable source. Please be sure to leave a review at the marketplace where you purchased this book. Your honest feedback is a valuable tool to help me with future books.

For more information on opportunities to play professional baseball, please check out the websites below.

Best of luck to your future!

James L. Gamble

www.gsbsports.com

www.mytimesports.com

www.ingramcontent.com/pod-product-compliance
Lightning Source LLC
Chambersburg PA
CBHW070633150426
42811CB00050B/280